Plant-based recipes for a conscious way of life

FARMACY KITCHEN

Created by
Camilla Fayed with Susie Pearl,
Emily Pearson and Pietro Cuevas

aster

For my Nana, Anisa Martinson, a talented Finnish oil painter whose love for cooking and flavour has inspired my culinary journey. Your eternally grateful Granddaughter.

An Hachette UK Company
www.hachette.co.uk

First published in Great Britain in 2018 by Aster, a division of
Octopus Publishing Group Ltd
Carmelite House
50 Victoria Embankment
London EC4Y 0DZ
www.octopusbooks.co.uk

ISBN 978-1-91202-350-9

A CIP catalogue record for this book
is available from the British Library.

Printed and bound in China

10 9 8 7 6 5 4 3 2 1

Consultant Publisher: Kate Adams
Senior Editor: Pollyanna Poulter
Copy Editor: Mary-Jane Wilkins
Art Director: Juliette Norsworthy
Photographer: Nick Hopper
Illustrator: Ella Mclean
Home Economist and Food Stylist: Sian Henley
Prop Stylist: Linda Berlin
Production Manager: Caroline Alberti

Disclaimer: We do not take responsibility for the accuracy of industry statistics or scientific reports around the health impact of organic food production and meat consumption. There is more information available on the Farmacy website with additional sources for finding out more.

Nutritional info recipe codes

✴
GF = gluten free

✴
NF = nut free

✴
R = raw

✴
VG = vegan

Contents

Foreword

Welcome to the Farmacy Kitchen where you will find inspirational ideas for conscious living and delicious recipes for plant-based eating that support both vegan and vegetarian diets. The Farmacy ethos aims to bring our attention back to nature, simplicity and balance. We love to follow the concept of 'simple abundance' in the food we create, using fresh, colourful wholefoods in inspired combinations for maximum flavour as well as easy digestion and enjoyment.

Farmacy London opened its doors in Notting Hill in 2016. The restaurant's mission is to offer a range of fresh, seasonal and nutritionally balanced plant-based food sourced from local, sustainable and environmentally conscious suppliers.

Life gets busy and it's often hard to find time to cook well at home and to balance the need for nutrition and flavour in our daily diet while avoiding processed food, sugar and animal products. Farmacy helps you to create this balance.

We know how good food tastes when it's made with love and intention. Cooking is a creative process and this books shows you how to make great-tasting food to nourish the body and energize the soul – a process you can bring to your own kitchen.

It's becoming more important than ever to think about the way we choose to eat and live, and the impact modern living is having on us, our planet and its natural resources. In this book you'll find new and helpful ideas on cooking well with plant-based food and how to make some important changes that will make a difference. We look at how a conscious way of living not only benefits individual health, but also communities, the environment and the world in general.

There is a list of essentials for your kitchen so that you have everything ready to cook well and we look at the best ways to bring in sustainable and affordable practices at home. Here is a collection of recipes that are straightforward whatever your level of cooking expertise. We are not trying to convert anyone. These are recipes that can be easily introduced to your diet and you don't have to be vegetarian to enjoy them.

I've been passionate about food since I was very young, but I haven't always eaten healthily. It has been a long journey for me, with many challenges, to enjoy eating a healthy, plant-based diet. The food I was eating in my teenage years and early twenties consisted largely of junk food. I ate a lot of processed food and regularly drank alcohol to be sociable. I put on weight, felt low in energy and had high cholesterol and other health issues as a result of poor nutrition. I was due for a wake-up call.

When I started a family, I realized that I had no choice but to put health and wellbeing at the top of my list of priorities. Being pregnant, I had to make some changes to the way I was choosing to live and eat. I knew that changing my diet and lifestyle could have a huge impact on how I felt on a physical level. The surprise was how it made me feel emotionally.

I was lucky to be able to travel to different places around the world to find out about new ways of eating and living.

I feel passionate about sharing this widely, passing on the information that I've learnt. My interest in growing food and biodynamic gardening increases as I find out more about the importance of where food comes from.

On this journey to healthier living, I've met some amazing people who have taught me so much. My thanks extend to all the teachers who have helped along the way and set me on this journey. I am filled with appreciation for those who pushed me to keep going when the mountain seemed too high to climb. This is an exciting time, when many people are coming together to enjoy plant-based eating with a shared intention to make better choices and live a healthier life.

Enjoy!
With love

Nature knows best when it comes to food, health and balance. Our approach is to create food that is delicious, good for the body and the Earth.

Farmacy Philosophy

An introduction

The world is waking up to the benefits of eating fresh, local ingredients that are grown and produced without harmful pesticides and without harm to animals. There is a strong shift in global consciousness with many people looking for more connection, kindness and compassion in life.

The recipes in this book use wholefoods, making good-tasting food that is naturally high in nutrients. At Farmacy we avoid processed ingredients and choose organic whenever possible to avoid ingesting the chemicals and pesticides used in non-organic food production. We do not use canned food or food that is clearly 'dead', instead opting for fresh and living food that is well sourced. Our recipes avoid using ingredients that can be high in genetically modified organisms (GMOs) such as corn, soy, potatoes and wheat.

In this chapter we outline our food philosophy and lay out the benefits of conscious eating – it makes a real difference. When we eat with awareness, the food tastes better somehow, we feel we are nourished in a deeper way, and our bodies digest more completely when we bring awareness to the process of eating. It is true that often this way of eating and living is considered a luxury, but more people than ever are becoming aware of their choices around food and conscious eating is becoming a familiar part of life.

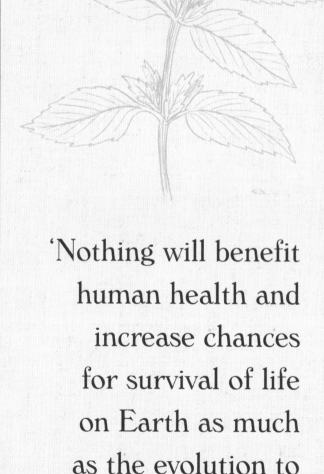

'Nothing will benefit human health and increase chances for survival of life on Earth as much as the evolution to a vegetarian diet.'

Albert Einstein

The four pillars

The Farmacy approach to conscious living and healthy eating
is based on four philosophical pillars: ancient wisdom, balance,
conscious positive intention and living without harming animals.

1. Ancient wisdom

Thousands of years ago, great philosophers from the lands of ancient Egypt and Greece talked about the idea of food as medicine. One of the earliest books ever discovered was found in ancient Egypt and contained recipes hand-written on scrolls of papyrus. These recipes used herbs, oils, plants and spices to cure ailments: the first prescriptions in recorded history. They were given up by the Egyptian philosophers as divine offerings to their gods.

Ancient Egyptians placed great importance and emphasis on being healthy and preserving health. Personal names and greetings used in everyday exchanges and letters reflected the culture's emphasis on wellness. Egyptian names were often formed using the word *seneb* which translates as 'healthy with vigour and strength'. Popular names for ancient Egyptians translate as 'I possess health' and 'May your father be healthy'. Many of the popular greetings of the day were based around the idea of wishing good health to others.

We have adopted some of this ancient wisdom in our philosophy and recipes using plants, herbs and spices in creative combinations to help maintain health and heal common ailments using food as medicine (*see* pages 18–27).

We also actively support farmers who follow the old principles of organic and biodynamic farming and who grow food in healthy, nutrient-rich soil, without using harmful chemicals and pesticides.

Organic farming combines traditional approaches to growing, supported with the latest farming technology, to benefit the environment and grow nourishing produce free from toxicity.

Biodynamic farms support a holistic approach of farming with the seasons and promote integration of all living organisms within the farm ecosystem – farmers, plants, animals and insects – all working together in rhythm with the seasons, just as our ancestors did.

2. Balance

To live well and be healthy, we need to find the right balance in all things. We need time to create, work, rest, play, eat well, exercise, get fresh air, spend time with others in our community, enjoy quiet time, support people, have fun and do all the things that give us a healthy life balance.

The recipes in this book are created with balance in mind: the food is designed to offer balanced nourishment that supports the body and mind, helping to create a healthy approach to nutrition and taking care of yourself.

3. Conscious positive intention

In recent years, there's been great interest in the power of the mind and the strong effects of setting out clear positive intentions. The mind is a mighty tool. This is something the ancients knew well and the secrets of using mind power were whispered and written about through secret societies for generations. Now this information is readily available and is becoming adopted and understood on a mainstream level.

Quantum physics has begun to explain through science what the ancients were saying thousands of years ago: thoughts are powerful and shape our experience in ways that are far stronger than we realize. The strength of our thoughts and intentions is much greater than many of us imagine.

The more we bring conscious awareness to the food we eat and the nature of the quality of that food, the more we build better understanding of our bodies, food habits, choices and relationships with each other and the planet.

'Day by day, what you choose, what you think and what you do is who you become.'

Heraclitus

4. Living without harming animals

The Farmacy philosophy is to enjoy a diet that does not cause suffering to animals. From an intuitive point of view, as well as from researching what is happening in the meat industry behind the scenes, we are taking a greater interest in the way we care for all animals.

Not only can practices followed within the meat industry severely impact the wellbeing of the planet, but the design of the human digestive system seems to suggest that animal protein is not meant for human consumption. Unlike carnivores, which have a short intestinal tract that allows meat to pass quickly through their system, our intestines are longer, like those of other plant-eaters, giving the body time to absorb the nutrients from plant-based foods. Eating meat is therefore linked to poor digestion in humans and means that we are more likely to ingest artificial hormones, chemicals, secondary toxins and parasites that can be found in meat products. Our bodies are designed to get all the nourishment they need without consuming meat or dairy. There are so many great alternatives available that transitioning to a meat-free diet has never been easier.

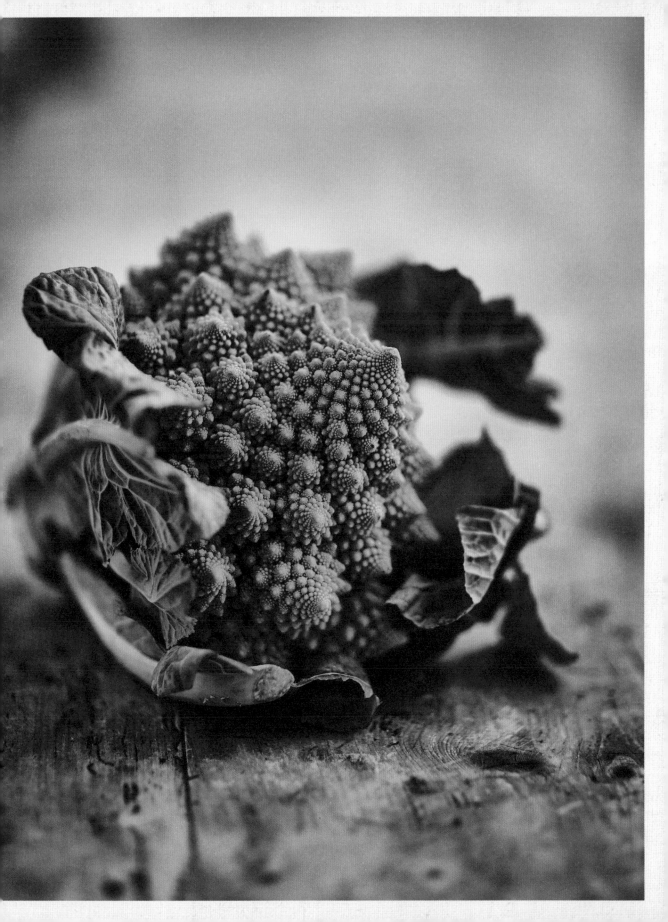

Good for you

Plant-based eating is wholesome, highly nutritious, ethical and sustainable. There are a range of health benefits to be gained from this type of eating; studies show that it can help in the prevention of some major illnesses and offers a more compassionate approach to the care of animals and the environment.

A well-rounded diet

An organic, plant-based approach to eating can provide all the nutrients needed for a well-rounded diet. For example, many people who eat a plant-based diet have higher intakes of the potassium-rich foods that help to reduce blood pressure, corresponding to a reduction in stress and anxiety, compared with those on other diets. It is possible to consume a broad range of healthy nutrients that fully support health and wellbeing without eating any meat, dairy products or refined sugar. There is a lot of data to support these findings.

Increased energy and wellbeing

We have high energy levels when eating natural wholefoods and following a plant-based diet. There are many world-leading sportsmen and women eating plant-based diets and excelling in sports that require physical stamina, energy and levels of peak performance.

Good gut health

A healthy gut is the fundamental basis of a healthy body, and many diseases begin in the gut. When we eat a varied diet high in fibre, with wholefoods such as grains, seeds and legumes, we can increase healthy gut bacteria, which in turn helps and supports the health and wellness of the whole body. Studies suggest that diets low in plants and high in animal products can significantly increase inflammation inside the body and disrupt the healthy flora of the gut.

'Wherever life plants you, bloom with grace.'

French proverb

... and good for the planet

A plant-based diet is also good for the health of the environment and kinder to animals. Growing plants has a less negative impact on the environment than raising animals for food. With a global shift away from farming livestock for food, we can reduce the impact of deforestation, greenhouse emissions and the erosion of natural resources. Animals enjoy life, rather than being raised in often terrible conditions before being slaughtered for food.

Cutting greenhouse gas emissions

Currently the food and farming industry accounts for at least ten per cent – and possibly as much as 33 per cent – of global greenhouse gas emissions. Leading scientists have acknowledged the positive role of organic farming both in tackling climate change and in securing a more sustainable food supply system that can provide food for everyone in the future. Soil stores carbon and organic soil stores more carbon than non-organic soil, contributing to the reduction in greenhouse gases needed to address climate change.

Avoiding chemicals and toxins fed to animals

Buying organic food and being mindful about food sources helps to cut down on ingesting poisonous chemicals and sprays that are widely used in mainstream food production. Consuming meat and animal products increases our exposure to dietary antibiotics, artificial hormones, industrial toxins, mercury, lead and other heavy metals. For example, a high proportion of people are now intolerant of cow's milk. Our intolerances to certain food groups are likely to be made worse by the many chemicals and medicines fed to dairy and other livestock and added to the food chain. There are many alternatives to consuming dairy products. At Farmacy we love making our own non-dairy milk, butter and yogurts (*see* pages 74–9).

Food as medicine

'Many diseases and illnesses can be correlated with thought patterns, lifestyle habits and quality of food choices.'
Dr Candace B Pert, *Molecules of Emotion*

Lifestyle and health

One of the exciting things about making healthy food is the alchemy that happens when ingredients are combined in a specific way, creating something that tastes amazing and unlike anything you've tried before.

Food fuels our bodies and provides the catalyst for the chemistry and biological transmissions that happen inside the cells and organs, providing us with the elements we need for energy creation and good health. The better the quality of fuel we give our bodies, the more good health, wellbeing and positive emotion we feel.

The intuition that ancient philosophers and traditional wellbeing systems such as Chinese medicine and Ayurveda had about the relationship between diet and health is once again coming to the fore as science explores this area. It is now accepted that the modern Western diet, high in processed foods and deficient in fresh wholefoods, is a major contributing factor to current levels of heart disease, cancer, diabetes and autoimmune diseases. Links are being discovered between diet and brain health, fertility and mental health.

Now that it is widely accepted that a poor diet has affected human health in a negative way, science is increasingly looking at the positive effects a good diet may have on our health and happiness, from the incredible anti-inflammatory properties of a spice such as turmeric, to the health-giving fermented foods that help replenish the good bacteria in the gut, essential to address many of the digestive issues that affect so many people today.

At the heart of new food science is the message that a plant-based, wholefood diet with little or no processed food is one of the best ways to improve our health. Including foods and cooking techniques that support digestion, and reducing foods that strain digestion, such as meat, sugar, dairy products and gluten, allows the body to absorb more nutrients and enjoy new levels of energy. This goes back to our theme of simple abundance – cooking and eating foods that have had as little interference as possible from farm to fork.

Food alchemy

The idea of food alchemy has been a core principle in putting together the recipes for this book. We've used alchemy to create the dishes, bringing together unique combinations of real foods, and we've also used only basic cooking techniques – roasting, boiling, baking and sautéing. That's it. It doesn't get any more complicated than these four basic cooking techniques. There is no point in making recipes too difficult. We do use a food processor and some basic kitchen gadgets, but essentially the recipe techniques are straightforward and easy.

Digestive health through alchemy of food

The alchemy of eating involves not just your food choices and the combination of foods you eat. It also means working with your body to eat complementary food groups that require the same sort of enzymes to digest the food effectively.

Good digestion

✓ Fresh organic vegetables and fruit are high in water, making them easily digestible.

✓ The fibre in plant-based food helps to move the food through the body, speeding up transit time through the gut, resulting in less fermentation and putrefaction in the intestine. This is good for preventing diseases and improving digestive health. We need plenty of fibre to stay healthy.

✓ Go for wholegrains rather than refined grains. Even if you're not allergic to gluten, gluten-free wholegrains such as quinoa, millet and teff are easier to digest and free from the potential allergens present in some glutinous grains, such as wheat, barley and rye.

✓ Eat food that helps your body produce healthy bacteria, including coconut yogurt and fermented foods such as kimchi, miso and sauerkraut, all of which contain plant-based probiotics. These help the body to produce good bacteria to keep the gut in best condition.

Bad digestion

✗ Processed food causes stress in the body and slows down digestion, depleting the body of nutrients and creating a feeling of low energy. The body takes nutrients from other places in the body to aid digestion. Processed food has a negative impact on the immune system too.

✗ Both red meat and processed food have been linked to digestive cancers, such as liver and colon cancer. Try to avoid both in a healthy, plant-based diet.

✗ Meat is hard to digest and can stay in the digestive tract for long periods because it lacks fibre and water. As a result, animal flesh may become stuck in the intestines as impacted faeces that can create toxicity inside the gut.

✗ Parasites are present in raw and undercooked meat and can cause disease and gut-bacteria deficiency. Many unhealthy parasites can enter the body through meat.

Making good food choices

✓ Be aware of what is being served and whether it contains meat or other animal products. Ask questions about the food you buy and eat.

✓ Get tested for food allergies and make changes to what you eat if necessary. Common allergens include gluten, dairy products, nuts and corn.

✗ Reduce or eliminate processed foods as far as possible.

✗ Cut down or out: caffeine, fizzy drinks, alcohol, deep-fried food, refined sugar, refined grains, canned food, junk food, meat, meat products, non-organic soy.

✓ Try mono meals from time to time – eating just one type of food at a meal – and see how it makes you feel and how much energy it gives you.

✓ Choose a plant-based diet.

Fruit

The body needs a lot of energy to process unripe fruit.
Fruit is packed with nutrients and contains high levels of fruit
sugar (fructose) so should be eaten in moderation. In other words, don't
assume that eating as much fruit as possible is a good thing. Including fresh,
ripe fruit in your diet is healthy in small amounts.

✓

Eat fruit when ripe.

✓

Sweet and acid fruits are best eaten separately to help you digest them better.

✓

Fruit should make up a maximum of 15 per cent of your daily food intake.

✗

Melons are high in sugar. Eat them on their own and not with other foods.

✗

Don't eat fruits and vegetables together – digesting them requires different
enzymes and the body digests them at different rates. Eating them at the same
time can lead to bloating and gas.

✓

When drinking fruit juice, dilute it with about 80 per cent natural,
filtered water to make the juice more digestible.

Fasting

Fasting has a powerful effect, improving all aspects of health – body, mind and spirit. Cutting out food for a cetain length of time allows the body time to naturally rest, rejuvenate and recharge itself. Fasting is part of the cultural and spiritual heritage of many countries around the world. It has a powerful and positive effect, regenerating and powering up the body's systems.

There are different approaches to fasting. Some people use liquid nourishment in the form of raw juices and whole juices; others only drink water. Do some research and find what is best for you and your body to give your stomach and digestion a rest and a chance to reset.

One-day fasts can cleanse the body and mind and help to restore energy levels and boost feelings of wellbeing. Stored toxins are released during a fast, the body can feel tired and achy and emotions can surface to be cleared. This is all part of the cleaning-out process. Take advice on how to fast and how to begin eating again after fasting. It's good to return slowly to eating, consuming a small quantity of light food to begin with to allow the digestion to come back to work gently. Fasting can make a real difference to your health and you will really appreciate the taste of good food again afterwards. If you have any medical concerns, always take advice from a doctor.

Research the right approach for you and test a few different methods to find the one that best suits you and your body.

Forgiveness
Acceptance
Self-control
Truth
Integrity
Nourishment
Grace

'I fast for greater physical and mental efficiency.'
Plato

Dairy detox

Dairy products are regularly genetically modified, unless certified organic. Factory-farmed cows are injected with antibiotics and growth hormones that enter the milk supply. Cows are often fed genetically modified grains grown using toxic pesticides and these easily transfer into milk and meat products. Humans are the only species who regularly and systematically drink another animal's milk.

Many dairy cows are kept in inhumane conditions that have an impact on the animal's health and the stress and fear they experience is likely to have an effect on the milk they produce. Drinking milk from mistreated cows that have been artificially inseminated to keep them lactating has an inevitable impact on human health and wellbeing. Many people are intolerant or allergic to dairy foods. We advocate moving away from dairy products and enjoying plant-based alternatives instead.

People often ask how they can consume sufficient calcium without eating dairy products. The dairy industry advertising campaigns of the past did a good job in establishing the belief that milk is essential for calcium and instilled the incorrect idea that milk is the only way to get enough in our daily intake. Calcium exists in many plants and seeds and it's straightforward to get the right daily levels of calcium from eating plant-based food.

In fact eating animal products leaches calcium from the body, but calcium can be found extensively through the plant kingdom in dark green leafy vegetables including spinach, kale, broccoli, watercress, mustard greens and seaweed. These foods all supply calcium to the body. Many legumes, nuts and seeds are also a good source of calcium, including lentils, chickpeas, white beans and black beans. Sesame seeds, for example, are rich in the mineral and are great for adding to salads and dishes. They form the base of the tahini that we use in many Farmacy recipes (*see* page 68). There are many easy ways to obtain calcium from eating plants.

'The time will come when men such as I will look upon the murder of animals as they now look upon the murder of men.'

Leonardo da Vinci

The Alchemy of Conscious Living

The more attention we pay to the way we live, the food we eat, the conversations we have, the choices we make, what we buy and how we treat the earth's resources, the more chance we have of making better and more empowering decisions that will lead to a healthier, more sustainable future for everyone. How we spend our time, who we spend time with, the ideas we think about, our actions and the words we speak – all these have a powerful impact on health and wellbeing.

Conscious eating

Conscious eating not only raises your awareness about what you are eating and putting into your body but also why, when and how you eat. In the rush of modern life, we have lost some of our natural connection with food and don't always take the time to notice what we are going to eat.

In conscious eating, you pause, taking the time to appreciate the food you are about to eat: you take a good look at it, smell it and feel some joy at the prospect of what you are about to eat, and then take your time to taste it consciously. This is an important part of digestion and helps us to power up the quality of good digestion. If you eat while watching your phone or catching up on messages, an important part of the natural digestion process gets missed.

Eating mindfully helps digestion and generates feelings of appreciation. When we eat with awareness, the food tastes better somehow; it feels as though we are nourished in a deeper way, and our bodies digest the food more completely. The first phase of digestion, called the cephalic phase, works best when the body is relaxed and when we pay attention to the process of eating.

Digestion and nourishment are improved when we become conscious of the process through smelling, seeing, tasting, chewing and swallowing. Through these instinctive processes, the body sends signals to the gut and digestive tract with detailed information that causes the release of the specific enzymes needed to break down the food that is on its way. The more consciously we eat, the better our digestion becomes.

Stress interrupts and slows down digestion significantly. If you suffer from poor digestion, bring awareness back by eating more slowly and consciously. It will make a big difference to your body's ability to assimilate food and nourish itself.

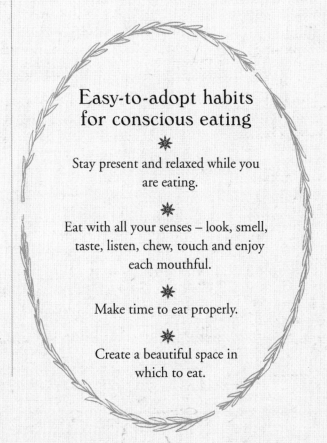

Easy-to-adopt habits for conscious eating

✳

Stay present and relaxed while you are eating.

✳

Eat with all your senses – look, smell, taste, listen, chew, touch and enjoy each mouthful.

✳

Make time to eat properly.

✳

Create a beautiful space in which to eat.

Digestion starts with a thought

Pavlov, with his dogs, was the first person to show in a scientific study that animals start salivating at the thought of a meal. In other words, they have a physiological digestive response due to thoughts alone. Since then, we have discovered that many physical digestive responses happen in the first stages of digestion, before any food reaches the stomach. These include salivation, secreting stomach acid and activating digestive enzymes to digest proteins, carbohydrates and fats.

Our experience of appetite is almost like a dance between the brain and the stomach, one signalling to the other to make us feel either hungry or satiated. Studies have shown that when eating mindfully, with awareness, physical feelings of satiation occur earlier than when eating without care and attention.

Stress and good digestion are opposites

The part of the nervous system which works in conjunction with digestion is the 'rest and digest' part of the system. A stress response causes the body to go into 'fight or flight', the opposite of the mode for digesting, taking the blood flow away from our digestive organs to the extremities, so we can flee if necessary.

Feeling stressed means that we don't produce the enzymes we need to tackle the food processing. The bottom line is that when we get stressed, digestion is significantly compromised. The best way to help your body absorb nutrients and digest food is to avoid stress, to focus on eating when you do eat and to avoid multitasking or eating on the run. Take your time and give eating the space it deserves. It's important to stay away from too many distractions, upsetting conversations, computer screens and anything that pushes our stress buttons, to be calm and relaxed to digest food fully and completely.

'Imagination is everything. It is the preview of life's coming attractions.'

Albert Einstein

Using all the senses

Using all our senses, and being aware of how they work together, is one of the secrets to optimal digestion. When we were recipe testing for this book, we had friends over to test and give feedback on the dishes we were creating. For one part of the trials, we asked the tasters to eat mindfully in silence and words of thanks were given before everyone started eating. There was a much greater appreciation of the food when eating silently and this was a profound effect but not surprising. Everyone said that they noticed more about the food. They noticed the colour, texture and feel of the dish and felt a sense of love for what they were eating. Every person reported that they appreciated the food offered far more than when they were engaged in discussions and that they felt much more gratitude for the food and one other.

Smell

Smell is a guide to effective digestion; it tells us if food is fresh or has gone bad. It creates a connection and an association with the emotional centre of the brain.

When we smell aromas we love, strong emotions are triggered and natural chemicals are released into the body. When our sense of smell is altered and we cannot smell easily, for example if we have a blocked nose from a cold, then our appetite and ability to taste food is affected. Good smell creates good digestion and makes the food so much more enjoyable. Our smell receptor, the nose, is located directly over the mouth – the perfect position to smell and approve the food we are about to eat.

Taste

When we are deciding what to eat, we tend to choose by focusing on a mix of the five main taste indicators – salty, sweet, sour, bitter and umami. In fact, we use all the senses in the complex process of choosing, eating and digesting food. Chewing food helps to develop the taste and appreciation of flavours that, in turn, sends information to the body to get it ready for action and digestion.

Umami is one of the five basic tastes, along with sweetness, sourness, bitterness and saltiness. It comes from a Japanese word meaning 'a pleasant, savoury taste'. We taste umami through taste receptors that recognize an amino acid called glutamate. This amino acid is found in many savoury foods, such as seaweed broths, shiitake mushrooms, green tea, fermented foods with bacterial or yeast cultures and nutritional yeast.

Scientists consider umami to be a distinct taste on its own, as we use specific receptors in our mouths to recognize this quality, rather than using a combination of other taste receptors to do so. Fermented sauces based on umami taste were used widely in ancient Rome and medieval cuisine and as early as the third century in China.

Umami was first discussed in 1908 by Kikunae Ikeda, a professor at Tokyo Imperial University. He noticed that the taste of *kombu dashi* (vegetarian stock used in Japanese cooking) was different from the tastes sweet, sour, bitter and salty. He named this new taste 'umami' and it's now used today to describe a fifth taste.

In the 1950s, scientists discovered that a greater and more intense umami flavour was created when foods that were rich in glutamate were combined with other foods containing ribonucleotides, such as shiitake mushrooms. When these foods are combined, they produce a deeper intensity of taste than each of the ingredients produces individually.

In our recipes, we use the alchemical principle of creating deeper and more intense flavours by combining certain ingredients.

Sight

The recipes in this book are colourful and designed to look beautiful. When we look at food, it triggers important physiological processes. The more colourful and fresher food looks, the more we want to eat it and the more we feel excited by it. The sensory receptors in our eyes do a great deal of work in triggering digestion. We can see whether food looks off and choose to steer clear if something doesn't look right or appetizing.

The way we see food and the amount of food on a plate is affected by the size and shape of the dishes it's served on. There's a phenomenon called the Delboeuf illusion. Studies have shown that bigger plates make a serving of food appear smaller, which results in people misjudging how much they eat. The sight of the food in relation to the size of the plate makes a difference in perception, so choose portion size and presentation carefully.

Harmonizing with the environment includes spending time making your food setting beautiful. At Farmacy we like to keep it simple and might set the tables with some fresh flowers, a pretty tablecloth or something from the garden representing the food and the season. Make beautiful crockery important in your arrangement. If everything works together it adds to the enjoyment of the food in a wonderful way.

Sound and touch

Chewing is important and listening to the crunch of textures gives the body important information that is decoded by the digestive messaging system, so chew and then chew more. It's easy not to chew food enough. We're often so busy rushing around that chewing well is often something we forget to do properly.

For digestion to work at its best, it's good to slow down the process and begin to be consciously aware of chewing. The more time we spend consciously chewing, the better the food is broken down by enzymes in the mouth, and chewing also allows enough time for the gut enzymes to do the job of assimilating the food's nutrients.

Conscious choices

An increasingly large percentage of everything we buy is discarded and goes to waste within 6 months of purchase, and most waste is not biodegradable. Bringing greater awareness to how we manage our rubbish is essential for a healthier and sustainable world.

We create billions of tonnes of waste every year and the quantity is rising. Rubbish and the way we manage the mountain of waste we produce is a big issue.

Say no to plastic

Plastic is a big problem for the health of planet Earth. Plastic litters cities, the countryside, the oceans and waterways and contributes to health problems for all living creatures, including humans and animals. Plastic pollution is a serious threat to the environment and plastic creates toxic exposure in every phase of its life cycle. Every year, millions of single-use cups and billions of plastic bottles are thrown away worldwide, and these numbers are rising fast. More food and products are covered in plastic than ever before.

Plastic does not fully degenerate. It breaks down into smaller pieces and is eaten by marine life, or it degrades into a form of plastic dust. Millions of marine animals and seabirds die every year as a result of eating or becoming tangled in plastic. Nearly every piece of plastic ever made and thrown away still exists, because there is no process or organism that can break it down fully.

When we store food in plastic wrapping or containers, chemicals can leach into food and create toxicity. In the restaurant, we avoid using plastic and choose biodegradable materials for our packaging and straws. We also employ eco-friendly solutions for cleaning, soaps and general kitchen use.

How to reduce your plastic footprint

✳

Say no to plastic bags; use reusable bags made
from eco-friendly material such as hemp.

✳

Buy fresh food from markets and local farm suppliers –
say no to non-biodegradable packaging.

✳

Do not buy plastic bottles. Get a water filter to improve
water quality at home and carry a reusable water canister.

✳

Say no to plastic straws when they are offered in restaurants and bars.

✳

Choose products packed in boxes rather than plastic bottles.

✳

Buy biodegradable rubbish bags and product packaging as
far as possible.

✳

Store food in glass containers, rather than plastic, to
prevent chemicals leaching into food.

✳

Look for the new wave of shops that encourage
customers to bring reusable containers from home
to fill up with staple ingredients.

Chemical-free farming

In the past, farming was carried out without using toxic pesticides and harmful chemicals. All food was organically grown – in other words, grown without chemical additives. From 1945, farmers began to add chemicals to the soil and sprayed them on plants to kill insects and creatures that ate the food crops during the growing season.

It has taken us decades to realize that chemicals that kill insects may not be good for humans either. We are now seeing the negative health effects of allowing these chemicals to become more established and part of the food chain over the last 60 years. Chemicals used in growing food enter the food through its skin and through the direct absorption of water in the soil. We are contaminating food from the inside out – washing the skin of vegetables and fruit helps but doesn't rid the food of all the chemicals that the food absorbs into its cells through the soil and skin membrane.

'If food is medicine, how we produce food is key. Farmacy is supporting agro-ecology and regenerative agricultural practices that remineralize the soil as well as helping support bio-diverse soil, to help us survive and thrive in a well-nourished society with a flourishing biosphere. It is in creating a diverse micro-biome in the soil that we begin to cultivate a civil society. We are truly civilized when we are well nourished.'

Emma Goodwin, biodynamic farmer

Much of the food grown by conventional methods is sprayed extensively, and many times, during the growing season to make it look good, keep insects away and to prevent blemishes on the skin, helping farmers sell it more easily. At Farmacy our food is organic wherever possible, and we buy food in its whole, raw form, sourcing regional and local produce – preferring to make everything in the house from scratch to make sure that it is high quality and free from chemical additives.

Pesticides uncovered

The pesticide industry is worth billions globally, and the big chemical companies that make pesticides and fertilizers have a great deal of power and involvement in many research studies. Some studies are partly funded by the biggest pesticide companies in the world, and these have excluded some very important effects on health for 'cost reasons'. If these negative health effects had been included in the studies, the results and outcomes would have been very different – and are likely to have compromised the reputation of the chemical corporates.

When we see images of people wearing gas masks and all-in-one protective overalls to keep them safe while spraying our crops, we need to start asking more questions about industry standards and the health problems caused by the widespread practice of coating the food and land with chemicals.

Soil quality

The nutrient quality of soil has become depleted and out of balance as a result of applying chemicals, while soil nutrient levels worldwide are reaching seriously low levels that are causing international concern. Agricultural industries around the world must pay closer attention to how to resolve the situation and make this a priority. Growing uncontaminated food in nutrient-dense soil is one of the most significant and pressing needs facing the world today.

Organic standards

Organic certification requirements vary in different countries. The general principles usually specify at least that:

- Land should not have been treated with toxic chemicals and fertilizers for three years prior to organic certification.
- Details of the methods and materials used in growing are recorded and monitored.
- No genetic engineering, irradiation or sewage sludge is allowed.
- Soil fertility and crop nutrients must be managed through specific cultivation practices.

Sustainability

Organic agriculture supports environmentally and economically sustainable food production and works closely with nature. Organic farming focuses on crop rotation and using animal manures, plant compost and bio-based pest control. When buying from organic growers, we know that food has been produced using fewer chemicals on the land. The water from farming goes directly into the waterways. Organic farming encourages wildlife and biodiversity.

Asking questions

When actively engaging in conscious living, it's important to know where food is grown: does it meet organic standards (including no pesticides) and is the quality of the soil it was grown in sustainable?

Natural beauty at home

At the end of this book we've included some natural beauty and home recipes to help you start making your own skincare range using ingredients with no added nasties or chemicals. Making all-natural cosmetics, skincare and house-cleaning products not only saves money, but also gives you the confidence of knowing that they are organic. Added to this you will have the pleasure of making them yourself with love in your own kitchen.

'Farmacy is the first place I have really enjoyed eating the food. As a biodynamic grower, I'm lucky to be eating fresh and tasty vegetables all year round and I'm usually disappointed by food when I eat out. There is so much thought and care around how to prepare food here so that it not only tastes good but also makes the body feel wonderful. I love the creativity and beauty of this food.'

Dorothea Leber, biodynamic farmer

In the Farmacy Kitchen

We share a handy at-a-glance list of ingredients and
store cupboard essentials. This section has all the
information you need for preparing nuts, seeds,
beans and grains as well as a simple guide on how to
grow your own sprouts. After the easy preparation,
it's quick to put together the recipes that follow
with the nourishing and activated ingredients.

Store cupboard essentials

Remember to choose organic products and to buy the best quality food possible. We like to use independent suppliers to support local businesses and organic food sources. Search out your nearest farm shops and health food stores. You will find that many of the ingredients here are now stocked either in supermarkets or health food stores. You can always build up your store cupboard over time as you try the recipes and become used to some of the less well known ingredients.

Kitchen staples

Bee pollen
Buckwheat groats
Cacao
Chia seeds
Chickpeas
Coconut, desiccated
Coconut, cold-pressed oil/butter
Coconut nectar
Coconut cream
Dates
Dijon mustard
Flaxseeds, whole (mill at home for best nutrients)
Goji berries
Hemp seeds
Honey (raw)
Maple syrup
Millet
Miso, brown rice (organic, GMO-free, gluten-free)
Mushrooms, dried, particularly shiitake

Mustard, organic Dijon
Nutritional yeast
Nuts: almonds, cashews, hazelnuts, macadamias, pecans, pistachios, walnuts
Oats (gluten-free)
Probiotic powder
Quinoa
Seeds: hemp, pumpkin, sesame, sunflower
Sea vegetables: dulse, kombu, nori, wakame
Tahini
Tamari (organic GMO-free)
Teff flakes

Herbs and spices

Asafoetida (optional: can be used when cooking beans)
Black pepper
Cayenne pepper or chilli flakes
Cinnamon
Cloves
Coriander
Cumin
Fennel seeds
Ginger
Nutmeg
Salt: sea salt, Himalayan pink salt and salt flakes (avoid regular table salt because it is often industrially produced and can contain unhealthy chemicals)
Turmeric

Flour
Buckwheat
Gram
Rice
Tapioca
Teff

Oils
Coconut, cold-pressed, virgin
Olive, cold-pressed extra-virgin
Sesame: regular and toasted
Sunflower

Vinegars
Apple cider
Rice
Sherry

Home and beauty
Activated charcoal
Bentonite clay
Peppermint oil (food grade)

Egg replacement

We use chia or flax seeds to
replace eggs in recipes. As a guide,
use 1 tablespoon of flaxseeds or chia
seeds mixed with 2½ tablespoons of
water to create a plant-based 'egg'.
Soak the seeds for 15 minutes and
you have a great replacement.

Sprouted
mung beans

Fruit chia jam

Fermented
kimchi

Sprouted
beans

Cashew
yogurt

Vegetable broth

Seaweed
broth

Tahini sauce

Nut milk

Green sauce

Nut butter

Seaweed

Rice

Dates

Philosopher's sauce

Alchemist's sauce

Borlotti beans

Salt

Fermenting kimchi

Farmacy seed mix

Butter beans

Walnuts

Sprouting mung beans

Olive oil

Kitchen equipment

A good-quality food processor
This is a good investment for a plant-based kitchen. Choose one with a range of attachments and a large bowl. An additional smaller bowl is useful for blending dips, dressings and sauces. They are expensive but will last a long time. Most good brands come with a guarantee of several years.

Blender
A high-speed blender does a different job from a food processor. Use it to blend juices, smoothies, soups or nut milks and to process nut flours.

Electric citrus juicer
This small gadget makes extracting citrus juice easy. It is fast, easy to use and simple to clean. Cut the citrus fruit in half, push one half on top of the juicer and it filters out the pulp and seeds in seconds. The juice is delivered into a glass below the spout: simple.

Electric whisk
A simple hand-held electric whisk is a useful addition and used in some of the recipes.

Sprouting jars
Buy a selection of sprouting jars to use for home sprouting. These are jars with a mesh lid made from muslin or loosely-woven fabric, allowing air to reach the sprouts and making them easy to drain.

Salad spinner
A good, old-fashioned salad spinner is a useful tool to clean and dry salads and sprouts. We wouldn't be without one in the Farmacy kitchen.

Nut milk bag
Choose a sustainable and compostable version made from hemp and cotton rather than a synthetic nut bag. These bags have a multitude of uses, as well as separating the pulp in nut milks: as a bag to hold herbs and spices when making soups and stews, for nut cheeses, as a colander for soft ingredients, or as a giant teabag to hold your favourite loose tea in a glass jar or teapot. Keep it handy, give it a rinse after use or put it in the dishwasher to clean it ready for the next job. We use nut milk bags every day.

Chopping boards
Choose wooden boards over plastic. Wash, rinse, dry and wipe with the cut side of half a fresh lemon to keep it fresh and sanitized.

Good knives
Investing in a set of knives with sharp blades will save you time, enable you to chop finely and make food preparation a breeze. Ceramic blades work well. Keep your knives in good condition with regular sharpening to help with precision cutting, which makes the food look good.

Mandolin
A useful gadget to evenly slice food into varying widths and thicknesses. Create slices, waffle cuts, crinkle cuts or dice firm vegetables and fruits. Choose one that is easy to clean and safe to use. Read the reviews, as there are different types and styles to choose from.

Pressure cooker

Pressure cookers are designed to reduce cooking times by up to half and to retain more of the nutrients in the food. For example, cooking beans in a pressure cooker reduces the cooking time from 2 hours to 20 minutes, and we all like to save time in the kitchen. The quality of these cookers has improved significantly in recent years and they're much easier to use than in the past. They are not essential, but help to save time and energy.

Strainers

Have fine and medium-gauge strainers in your kitchen and choose strainers made from a non-plastic and eco-friendly material.

Flasks and water bottles

Keep a selection of food-grade stainless steel flasks and reusable water bottles at home. These are great for carrying drinks on the go. They keep drinks fresh and mean you don't need to buy water in plastic bottles. Check that there are no plastic liners in the flask that might leach chemicals into your drinks.

Storage containers

Glass or food-grade stainless steel containers are best for storing, freezing and carrying food. Traditional plastic containers can transfer chemicals – such as bisphenol A (BPA) – into food. We recommend avoiding plastic containers for storage, staying BPA-free (look at labels when buying), and choosing glass or food-grade metal storage. Avoid using aluminium foil for cooking and wrapping food. Wrapping food in foil and then heating it, especially if it is acidic and spicy food at a high temperature, can cause leaching of aluminium into the food. Head for non-plastic and non-aluminium alternatives and use paper bags to store food and greaseproof paper for baking and wrapping food.

Water filter system

The quality of tap water varies significantly depending on where you live. Tap water can contain fluoride, chlorine, pesticides and heavy metals in varying amounts. It's worth checking the quality of your water (there are cheap kits available to do this) and consider water filters or tap filter systems to improve it.

Cookware

Reducing your exposure to toxins and staying free from chemicals means paying attention to the pans you use in the kitchen. Take a close look at the quality and materials of your cooking pans. Look for eco-friendly and 'green' ware when choosing a healthy range of pans.

Ceramic cookware is a healthy choice. Ceramic enamelled cast-iron cookware is popular and versatile. These pots can go from the stove top to the oven and have a good non-stick surface. When cleaning, take care not to chip or scratch the surface. Clay crock pots are great for roasting. They retain heat after cooking and keep food warm on the way to the table. Always check if the glazes used on the pots contain toxins such as lead. Read the label and research the quality of your cooking pots carefully.

Some people say that stainless steel saucepans are safe and others believe that if you use them to cook acidic food, they can leach nickel, cobalt and chromium into the food. Nickel is present in stainless steel and can cause allergies. To test if it's present, take a magnet and check how magnetic the pan is. The more magnetic it is, the less nickel is present.

Glassware is safe and non-toxic to use. Glass is not as good a conductor of heat as ceramic, but it is toxin free and safe to use for cooking.

Avoid aluminium; this is not a safe material for cooking. It has been linked to Alzheimer's and dementia. When heated, aluminium leaches into food easily, especially when cooking acidic foods. Some pans have an aluminium core inside a safer metal because it heats up quickly. The problem is that if the surface is damaged, food can be exposed to aluminium. It's best to avoid cooking food in any pan that contains traces of this metal. Copper pans are also best avoided as studies show that copper can leach out and using them for cooking may mean consuming more than the recommended daily dose, which can be harmful.

Teflon became popular as it prevents foods from sticking. It's easy to scratch and if damaged the surface layer of Teflon can get into the food and be ingested along with it. Scratched Teflon can reveal the surface underneath which is often a harmful metal such as aluminium. Teflon releases toxic fumes when heated and it's not advisable to breathe these in or absorb them into the body

Plastic should not be used when cooking. When heated or microwaved, the toxic chemicals it contains go straight into food and have negative effects on health. Many plastics leach xenoestrogens or BPA when heated. These are artificial hormones that cause hormonal imbalances. This is why you should never heat a plastic container or put hot food or liquid into plastic bowls. Reheating fast food in plastic containers or ready meals bought in a plastic tray may leach chemicals and toxins into the food and this is not a healthy method of heating.

Preparing nuts, seeds, grains and beans

Nuts, seeds, grains and beans offer some of the best sources of essential nutrients, including vitamins, dietary fibre, healthy fats and proteins. We use them regularly in the Farmacy kitchen to create nutrient-rich dishes, crunchy textures and creamy sauces.

Activating nuts and seeds by soaking makes them a much more potent source of vitamins and nutrients. When raw nuts and seeds come into contact with water, they come alive and shoots begin to grow. Many varieties have enzyme inhibitors to protect them from damage in their early stages of growth. These inhibitors slow down the natural absorption of nutrients and are neutralized by the soaking stage, making the nuts and seeds more nutritious and easier to digest. Traces of dust or tannins are washed away during soaking, making them taste better too.

As a general guide, denser nuts need longer soaking. But do take care not to soak them for longer than the recommended time (*see* chart below), as this can compromise the flavour, texture and nutritional benefits.

Soaking is best done at room temperature. For most nuts, the easiest way to do this is to soak them overnight and rinse and strain them in the morning.

The nuts and seeds we love to use give a great range of flavours and they are highly versatile. Cashews add a creamy, mild taste to dishes; almonds are bursting with nutrients and have a health-boosting alkalizing quality; while walnuts are known as 'brain food' because of their high levels of omega-3.

Soaking nuts

Almonds	overnight	Raw almonds contain more nutrients than any other nut, including vitamin E, calcium, phosphorus, iron and magnesium. They also contain zinc, selenium, copper and niacin and can be ground into flour.
Cashews	1–2 hours	These have no enzyme inhibitors, so need less soaking. They contain monounsaturated fats, iron and minerals, including copper, magnesium, thiamine, calcim and niacin. They are high in starch, making them good for dips, creams and as a thickening agent.
Pecans	4–6 hours	Contain more than 19 vitamins and minerals, including vitamins A and E, calcium, magnesium, potassium and zinc. Just 25g (1oz) provides about 10 per cent of daily recommended fibre intake.
Walnuts	1–2 hours	Have a high concentration of omega-3 fats and antioxidants.

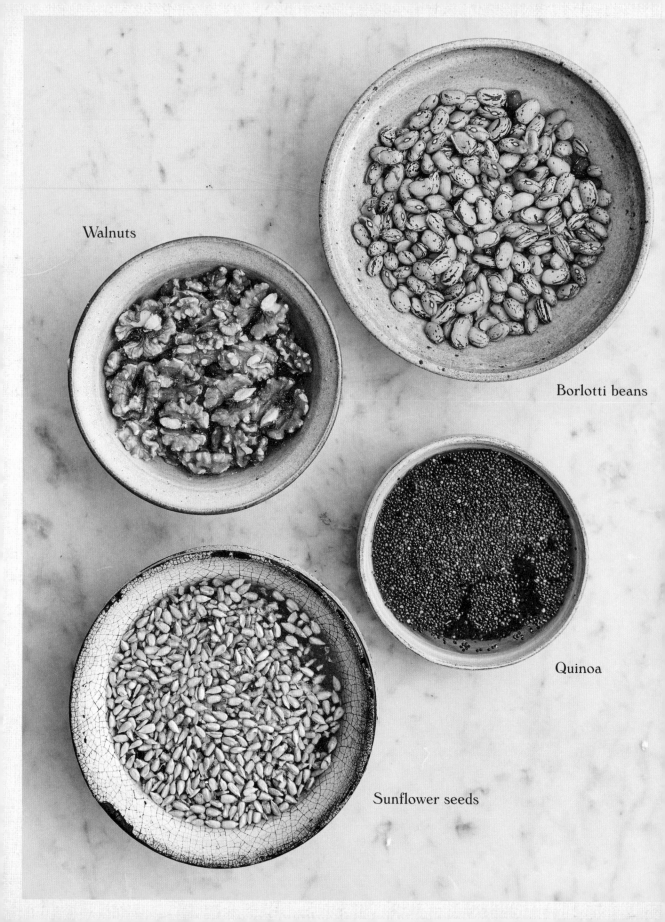

Walnuts

Borlotti beans

Quinoa

Sunflower seeds

Soaking seeds and grains

Buckwheat	Flaxseed	Millet	Quinoa	Rice	Sunflower	Teff
8–12 hours	8 hours	8–12 hours	8–12 hours	8–12 hours	4 hours	8–12 hours

The cooking time of grains is shorter if they have been soaked. Soaking also makes the grains more easily digestible and nutritious.

To soak the grains, use 185g (6½oz) of grain to 2 tablespoons of lemon juice or a flavourless vinegar (or use less depending on how much you like an acidic taste) and add warm water.

Put the grains, juice or vinegar and water into a saucepan and soak overnight.

The longer the grains soak, the less water is needed and the shorter the cooking time required. Reduce the water specified on the packet by 25 per cent and also the cooking time by 20 per cent if you have soaked the grains.

After soaking, rinse the grains thoroughly until the water runs clear. They are then ready to cook.

Cooking seeds and grains

	Buckwheat	Millet	Quinoa	Basmati rice	Brown rice	White rice
Water (ml)	120ml	355ml	355ml	295ml	530ml	235ml
Cooking time (minutes)	5	10–15	10–15	20	35	15
Resting time (minutes)	20	20	20	20	20	20

The cooking times in the chart above are for 180g (6oz) of dry grains. Be sure to add ¼ tablespoon salt to the water before cooking.

The grains will need some time to fully absorb the liquid once you take the saucepan off the heat. Leave the lid on and let the pan sit, covered, for 20 minutes. You will have perfectly cooked grains if you allow them to absorb all the liquid.

Dry roast the soaked millet before cooking, by stirring it in a pan over a medium heat until it smells toasted, to get loose grains which don't clump together.

Activating nuts and seeds

Rinse the nuts or seeds, put them in a large glass bowl or jar and add water. Cover with a lid or light cloth and soak for the time specified on the soaking chart (*see* pages 49 and 51). Then rinse again and store in the fridge for one or two days.

Dehydrating nuts

Preheat the oven to its lowest setting, spread the nuts out on a baking tray and bake them for several hours. Alternatively, put them in a dehydrator for 24 hours, until they are crisp. When nuts have been activated and dehydrated, they can be kept in a sealed container in a dry and dark place for several months. If the nuts are not completely dried out first, they can develop mould, so it is important to make sure that they are completely dried.

Making nut flour

It's easy to make nut flour at home. Good nuts for making flour are almonds, cashews and hazelnuts. Make sure the nuts are fresh and use blanched almonds for flour or it will become almond meal.

Put the nuts into a blender, grinder or food processor and whizz them for 8–10 seconds until the mixture has the texture of flour. Make sure not to over blend and stop before the nuts become too much like butter in consistency.

Store in a dry, sealed container in a dry, dark place.

A note on nut allergies

❋

Some people experience serious allergic reactions to nuts. It's important to check for nut allergies when preparing food for a group and ask about any possibility of nut intolerance.

Sprouting

Sprouts are 10–30 times more nutritious than vegetables. They are one of the most nutritious of all wholefoods and full of flavour. By ingesting sprouts as living food, you take the energy from the shoots directly into your body. At the sprouting stage, plants have the strongest concentration of nutrients in their life cycle. Sprouts are easily digestible because of their delicate cell walls.

Sprouts are easy and cost effective to grow at home. There are many advantages to home sprouting. As the sprout grower, you know they are chemical-free. It doesn't take long to start sprouting at home and you will have access to living food packed with nutrients all the year round. When you add water to the seeds, they begin to sprout small shoots as they move into the growing phase. During the first few days of sprouting these little shoots are at their most potent and nutritionally dense stage, bursting with enzymes, vitamins and minerals.

How to sprout

Take a large preserving jar with a metal lid that can hold a muslin cloth cover, or use a glass jar and cover it with a clean cloth. Place the seeds in the bottom of the jar and put the cover on. Pour three times more water than you have seeds through the cloth, swirl the seeds, drain and discard the water. Cover again with fresh water. Soak overnight.

Next day, rinse the seeds in water, swirl and drain again. Continue to rinse, swirl and drain over the next few days until small white sprouts appear. During hot weather, you may need to rinse and drain the seeds two or three times a day. The sprouts will continue to grow until they have filled the jar.

Dry the sprouts as thoroughly as possible (use a salad spinner if you have one). If they are stored wet, they will spoil quickly. Keep them in the fridge, ideally in an airtight container. Make a note of the date and mark an end date for using them on the jar to make sure you eat them fresh. They will last 7–10 days when stored correctly.

These steps only take a couple of minutes a day, and will give you plenty of living, delicious and nutritious sprouts ready to eat. Sprout heaven!

Soaking and sprouting times

	Soaking time	Sprouting time
Alfalfa	5 hours	5 days
Broccoli	8 hours	4 days
Chickpea	12 hours	3 days
Fenugreek	6 hours	5 days
Lentil	8 hours	3 days
Mung bean	8 hours	3–5 days
Quinoa	6 hours	1–2 days
Radish	6 hours	5 days
Sunflower	6 hours	24–48 hours

Mung beans, soaking

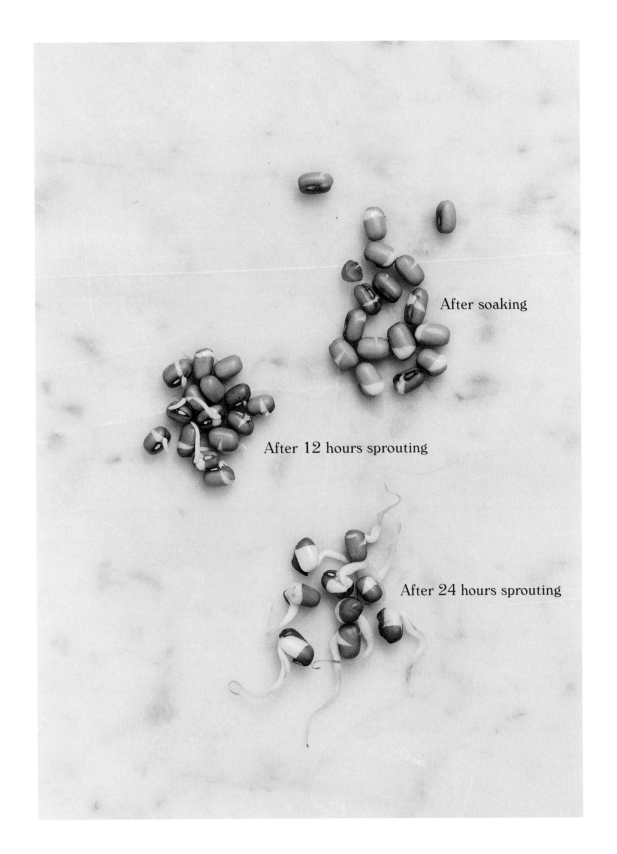

After soaking

After 12 hours sprouting

After 24 hours sprouting

Cooking with beans and pulses

We love using beans, pulses and legumes in our recipes. Steer clear of the canned varieties to avoid preservatives and soak and cook your own. This guide tells you all you need to know about handling beans and pulses as well as giving you some of our best bean hacks.

Different beans have different soaking and cooking times (*see* chart right). It takes a few hours to cook beans in a regular saucepan. You may like to use a pressure cooker as this reduces the cooking times.

Choose organic and buy in bulk where you can from stores supporting a no-waste policy which allows you to take your own refillable container. Check that the beans are fresh and do not look wrinkly. When they are more than 12 months old, beans begin to lose their fresh taste. If you aren't sure about the age of beans, ask your grocer to place a special order.

Soaking beans is important. It reduces the cooking time and helps the body digest them more easily. You may need to build up the enzymes required to help your body digest beans well. Start by eating small legumes (lentils, aduki) and when you can digest these easily, move up to a medium-size bean such as black or pinto beans. Then move on to bigger ones, such as red kidney beans and chickpeas.

Eating a lot of beans and pulses can result in extra air and gas in the body. Beans contain a sugar called oligosaccharide. Humans lack the enzyme required to break down this sugar. When it arrives in the lower intestinal tract, it can ferment and this causes the build-up of gas. The gas isn't absorbed into the intestine, and the body has to expel it, creating that not-so-lovely gassy effect.

To stop the gas when eating beans, start by laying out the dry beans and sorting them for quality, discarding any stones and dried out or discoloured beans. Put the beans in a container, pour over water and leave them to soak to allow the beans' sugar to be released. Change the soaking water a few times to prevent the sugar being reabsorbed into the beans.

Cook the beans in fresh, clean water, adding ½ onion, ½ tablespoon of salt and a bay leaf. Add two pinches of the spice asafoetida (from a local Indian spice stockist), or baking soda or a 10cm (4in) piece of kombu (a kelp) to the water. This helps to break down the sugar further and avoid the gas. Skim off the foam from the top during cooking. The beans are fully cooked when completely soft. Most beans will need a second cooking to create some of the dishes in the recipes.

The exception to this is lentils, which can become mushy if cooked for too long and should only be cooked once. Cook lentils according to the guidelines on the right, adding chopped carrots and celery to give more depth of flavour. Add peppercorns and Farmacy Seed Mix (*see* page 80) and an equal volume of liquid to lentils.

Aquafaba

Aquafaba is the common name for the cooking liquid from beans and legumes, which is usually thrown out after the cooking process. It contains a unique mix of starches, proteins and other soluble plant solids that have dissolved during cooking. Aquafaba is very versatile, and has a wide range of uses, including emulsifying, foaming, binding and thickening. It can be used to replace egg whites in many recipes too, such as in our Alioli (*see* page 114).

Bean soaking and cooking times

Type of dried bean, 200g (7oz)	Soaking time	Regular cooking time	Pressure cooking time
Black	4–6 hours	45–60 minutes	15–20 minutes
Chickpeas	Overnight	1½ –2½ hours	15–20 minutes
Lentils	1–2 hours	20–30 minutes	Not recommended
Mung	Overnight	15 minutes	Not recommended
Split mung	30 mins	8–10 minutes	Not recommended
White	Overnight	45–60 minutes	4–5 minutes

Tips

Soaking and cooking times vary for different
kinds of bean. If you're using more than one
kind of bean in one dish, cook them separately.

You can use the cooled cooking water to
water the houseplants – they love bean
water (if unsalted).

Be sure to boil and skim the froth from
the beans before using a slow cooker
or pressure cooker.

In this section, you'll find a range of basic recipes that we use regularly at home. We suggest you start by making these and keep them to hand in the kitchen. Many of them store well and they will all give you a great starter kit for the dishes that follow. With these basics prepared, you're good to go.

Basics

Vegetable Broth

This golden broth is full of goodness and forms the basis of many dishes in our kitchen. In it, vegetables and spices come together to create a deep flavour and provide good nutrition. This broth is an elixir that packs a big hit of vitamins and minerals with a slightly spicy kick. It's also delicious as a broth on its own and you can add your favourite spices to enjoy on a cold winter's day.

Quantity: 1.2 litres (2 pints)
Preparation time: 20 minutes

1 celery stick, cut into 4

2 onions, quartered

1 carrot, quartered

1 turnip, quartered

1 fennel bulb, including the fronds, quartered

2 tbsp olive oil

1 head of garlic, halved horizontally

1 slice of fresh root ginger, about 1cm (½in) thick

3 cloves

1 bay leaf

6 black peppercorns

1 bunch of parsley stems

1.5 litres (2½ pints) water

1½ tbsp salt

Put all the ingredients into a saucepan over a medium heat and bring to the boil. Reduce the heat and simmer gently for 15 minutes, then turn off the heat. Strain off the liquid and use as necessary.

This broth can be stored in an airtight container and chilled for 3–4 days or frozen.

Seaweed Broth

Farmacy Seaweed Broth is inspired by an ancient Japanese recipe. It's a highly nutritious, mineral-rich base that is a great way to add depth of flavour without using fats or additional salts. We use it in a range of recipes, including Philosopher's Sauce and many soups. It's also used to soak chia seeds to give extra flavour to the Farmacy Caesar Salad (*see* page 156).

Quantity: 1.2 litres (2 pints)
**Preparation time: 30 minutes,
    plus 1 hour soaking**

2 pieces of dried kombu, each about
    15cm (6in) long, soaked overnight
    in 1.2 litres (2 pints) water
4 dried shiitake mushrooms
½ tbsp salt

Put the soaked kombu and its soaking water into a saucepan over a medium heat and slowly bring to the boil. Just before the water boils remove the kombu (it's important not to boil kombu or it will become bitter). Keep the kombu, as it can be reused one more time before needing to be discarded.

When the water boils, reduce the heat to low and add the shiitakes. Cook for 1 minute, skimming the surface, then turn off the heat. Let the saucepan stand for an hour, then strain the broth.

Store for up to a week in a sealed jar in the refrigerator, or freeze.

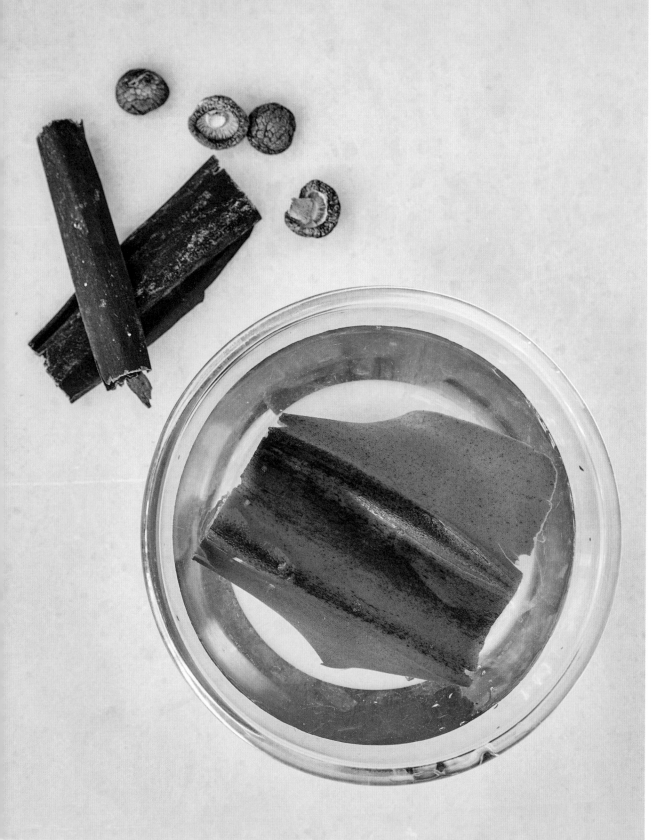

Philosopher's Sauce

Philosopher's Sauce is Farmacy's take on classic Asian fish sauce. It's a great way to add a deep umami taste to dishes such as Thai curries and noodles. This is a highly nutritious base which we use in a range of Farmacy recipes and has all the goodness of Seaweed Broth and black garlic combined.

Quantity: 250ml (9fl oz)
Preparation time: 15 minutes

500ml (18fl oz) Seaweed Broth (*see* page 61)
1 black garlic clove, crushed
2 garlic cloves, crushed
1¼ tbsp salt
60ml (4 tbsp) tamari
1 tsp sherry vinegar

Place all the ingredients in a saucepan, bring to the boil, then reduce the heat to a simmer and reduce the liquid to half the amount. This will take about 15 minutes.

Store in a dark, dry cupboard for up to three months. This sauce doesn't need to be refrigerated.

Green Sauce

Our magic Green Sauce is a raw sauce inspired by 'schug' or 'zhug', a hot chilli sauce of Yemeni origin which packs a punch of flavour whenever it is added to a dish. We use Green Sauce for a flavour lift in salads and other dishes, such as Aubergine Rolls (*see* page 120). It mixes well with Tahini Sauce (*see* page 168) as the flavours complement one another. Chillies contain fibre and a range of vitamins and minerals, including iron, magnesium, potassium, copper and manganese. The coriander and lemon aid digestion and help support the immune system.

Quantity: 250ml (9fl oz)
Preparation time: 5 minutes

2 garlic cloves
1–2 green or jalapeño chillies
1 tsp Farmacy Seed Mix (*see* page 80)
1 large bunch of coriander, stems and leaves
125ml (4fl oz) sunflower or rapeseed oil
2 tbsp lemon juice
½ tsp salt

Put the garlic, chillies and seed mix in a food processor and blend together. Add the coriander, oil, lemon juice and salt. Process until the sauce is smooth, like pesto. Check the seasoning and adjust if necessary with more lemon juice.

Keep in an airtight container in the refrigerator for up to 1 month. The colour may darken over time due to oxidation, but this doesn't affect the flavour. You can top with a thin layer of oil to prevent oxidation, or alternatively, freeze half to use another time.

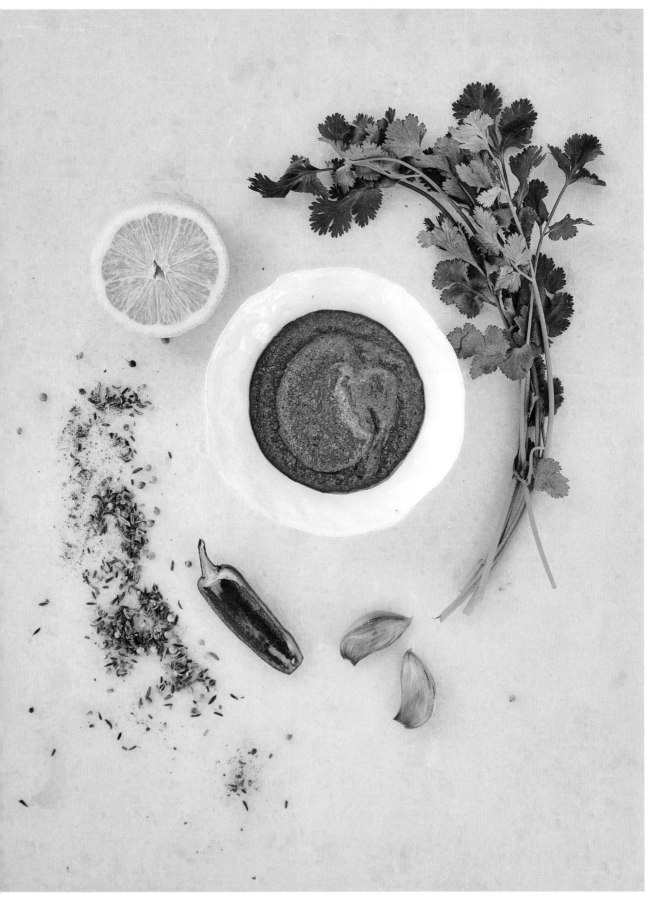

Tahini Sauce

GF NF R VG

Use this versatile, oil-free sauce however you fancy. It is one of our favourites in the Farmacy kitchen range and mixes well with Green Sauce (*see* page 66) for a flavour made in heaven. It's rich in protein and minerals, including magnesium, potassium and iron. We use it as a creamy, nutritional hit in many of our dishes and love loading it on to salads or adding it as a topping to fresh vegetables.

Quantity: 550ml (1 pint)
Preparation time: 5 minutes

250ml (9fl oz) tahini
125ml (4fl oz) lemon juice
½ tsp salt
175ml (6fl oz) water

Mix the tahini, lemon juice and salt in a blender and gradually add the water to create the desired consistency.

Keep in a screw-top jar in the refrigerator for up to a week.

Alchemist's Sauce

GF NF R VG

This is one of our main sauces which we use to add depth of flavour. It tastes similar to Worcestershire sauce and is full of natural goodness. We use Alchemist's Sauce in our Caesar Salad dressing (*see* page 156) and as a special ingredient in the raw courgette dressing of the Farmacy Macro Bowl (*see* page 164). This wonderful sauce adds a new level to the umami of plant-based food preparation. It tastes great in a Bloody Mary, too!

Quantity: 320ml (11fl oz)
Preparation time: 5 minutes

250ml (9fl oz) apple cider vinegar
60ml (4 tbsp) tamari
1 tbsp coconut nectar
½ date, soaked for 30 minutes
¼ tsp ground ginger
1 coin-sized piece of fresh root ginger
¼ tsp Dijon mustard
1 tbsp thinly-sliced onion
1 garlic clove, crushed
¼ tsp ground cinnamon
¼ tsp black pepper
¼ tsp coriander seeds
¼ tsp fennel seeds
½ tsp tamarind sauce

Place all the ingredients in a screw-top jar, replace the lid and shake vigorously. Shake it again. Leave for 30 minutes to allow the flavours to develop, but no longer or the garlic will begin to overpower the other flavours. Strain off the liquid and transfer to a glass bottle with a lid.

Keeps for up to 3 months. This sauce does not need to be refrigerated.

Fruit Chia Jam

GF NF R VG (if using maple syrup)

This is a healthy chia jam to spread on toast, add to desserts or top a probiotic yogurt breakfast. It has no refined sugar and a fresh and fruity flavour. Chia seeds are full of fibre, proteins, omega-3 fatty acids and many other nutritional goodies. They are great for the digestion, too.

Quantity: 125g (4½oz)

Preparation time: 5 minutes, plus 30 minutes chilling

100g (3½oz) fresh fruit, peeled and pitted as necessary (we used mango, blackberry and raspberry)

2 tsp honey or maple syrup

2 tsp lemon juice

2 tsp chia seeds

Place the fruit in a blender with the honey or maple syrup and lemon juice. Blend until it reaches a soft and jammy consistency.

Stir in the chia seeds. Put in the refrigerator for 30 minutes to allow the chia seeds to expand.

Store in an airtight container in the refrigerator for up to 7 days.

Almond Butter

This recipe is a one-ingredient wonder that transforms almonds into a luxurious, velvety spread. We use it as a butter replacement in our recipes and in a variety of plant-based dishes. Almonds are high in vitamin E and are one of the most nutritional of all nuts. The butter adds flavour and thickens sauces with all the nutty goodness that almonds provide.

Quantity: approx 250g (9oz)
Preparation time: 20 minutes, plus 15 minutes cooking

500g (1lb 2oz) raw, peeled almonds, unsoaked

Preheat the oven to 150°C (300°F), Gas Mark 2. Place the almonds on a baking tray and put in the oven for 15 minutes. Be careful not to colour the nuts too much; do not fully toast them.

Place the nuts in a food processor and process at high speed for 2 minutes. Reduce to medium speed and process until the mixture has a creamy, tahini-like texture, and is smooth and velvety. If there are still lumps, continue processing.

The mixture will go through different states, turning from almond meal to powder and then into butter. Be patient and scrape the bowl frequently, especially at the start. The time it takes will vary depending on the freshness of the nuts – this process can take up to 15 minutes.

Notes

This is one recipe for which you don't need to soak the almonds. The almond butter works best when the nuts' natural oils are warmed, allowing them to be released more easily.

This recipe does not work with ready-ground almonds. Raw, peeled almonds produce a creamy and velvety butter texture free of the solids of the skin. Alternatively, you can use almonds with their skins to create a darker butter with a slightly different flavour.

This keeps well in an airtight container in a dry, cool place.

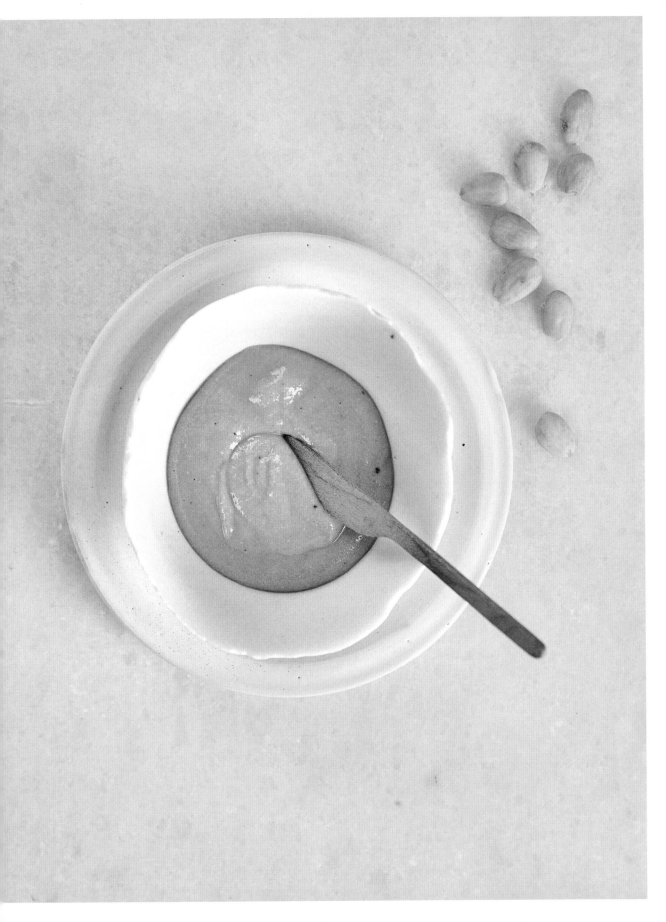

Cashew Yogurt

This probiotic-rich yogurt can be eaten alone, used to make sauces or added to dishes as a creamy, good-looking garnish. This makes a large jar of delicious yogurt that helps to keep the gut healthy, maintaining gut flora and enhancing general wellness.

Quantity: 700ml (1¼ pints)

Preparation time: 10 minutes, plus 2 hours soaking, plus 24–36 hours fermenting

225g (8oz) unsalted raw cashews, soaked

300ml (10fl oz) water

¼ tsp probiotic powder or 2 probiotic capsules

¼ tsp vanilla powder (optional)

1 tbsp honey or maple syrup (optional)

pinch of salt (optional)

Drain and rinse the cashews, then place them in a blender with the water and probiotic powder or capsules. Blend until smooth with a custard-like consistency.

Place the yogurt in a clean, lidded jam jar and cover with a clean tea towel or muslin cloth. Leave some space at the top of the jar for the yogurt to develop without overflowing.

Keep in a warm place (try the top of the refrigerator) for 24–36 hours. The longer you leave the jar undisturbed, the tangier the yogurt will be. It's ready when the mixture appears foamy and comes away from the sides of the jar. It should have a strong and pleasant, tangy aroma.

When the yogurt has fermented, return it to the blender and blend again, adding the optional ingredients, if using.

Transfer to a glass container with a lid and store in the refrigerator.

This keeps in the refrigerator for up to a week.

Nut & Seed Milk

GF NF (if made with seeds)
R VG

Nut milks are a versatile and healthy way to have milk without eating dairy products. Use them on breakfast cereals, in drinks, to add creaminess to smoothies and as a healthy base for sauces and purées. This is a highly nutritious milk full of protein and goodness. If you get into the habit of soaking nuts every night, you can quickly whizz up some fresh nut milk each morning.

Quantity: 1 litre (1¾ pints)
Preparation time: 10 minutes, plus soaking time

150g (5½oz) nuts or seeds, soaked (*see* soaking chart, pages 49 and 51)
1 litre (1¾ pints) water
½ tsp vanilla powder (optional)
1 tbsp coconut oil (optional)
2 tbsp sweetener or 3 pitted dates (optional)
pinch of salt (optional)

Rinse and drain the soaked nuts or seeds thoroughly. Put in a blender with the water, blend, then strain through a nut milk bag or cheesecloth into a bowl.

Clean the blender. Return the milk to the blender with the optional ingredients, if using.

This keeps in an airtight jug in the refrigerator for 3–5 days.

Note

Cashew nuts have no skin so they don't need to be strained.

78 BASICS

Farmacy Seed Mix

The Farmacy Seed Mix takes food way beyond classic seasoning. It deepens flavours, taking dishes to a new level. This mix pops up in many recipes. Make a batch and keep it in the kitchen to use as needed. This recipe was inspired by chef Peter Gordon. We use it frequently in the Farmacy kitchen.

Quantity: 6 tbsp
Preparation time: 5–10 minutes

2 tbsp each cumin, coriander and
    fennel seeds

Put the seeds in a dry frying pan without oil over a medium heat and cook them until they are fragrant. This takes about 3 minutes. The aim here is not to toast the seeds, but to release the beautiful combination of flavours by warming the seeds together in the pan.

Put the seeds in a food processor and pulse and blend until they have a consistency you like.

Store in an airtight container in a dry, dark place for up to 6 months.

Here's a range of great ways to begin the day in Farmacy style. There's porridge, a smoothie bowl, seed bread and a feast of other good, nourishing breakfast dishes to kick-start your day in a healthy way.

Breakfast

Soothing Porridge

GF NF (if pistachios not used)
VG (if honey not used)

Millet is one of the best-kept health-food secrets. It's high in nutritional value and has been eaten by many ancient cultures for centuries. The flavour is deliciously nutty and surprisingly creamy when cooked. It's also gluten-free. This version of porridge is a great alternative to the more common seeds and grains. It is a good source of protein, calcium, iron, zinc, magnesium and essential fats, helping to support heart health, protecting from diabetes, improving digestion and detoxifying. With the addition of ginger, turmeric, vanilla and cinnamon, it's also anti-inflammatory and full of antioxidants.

Serves 2

Preparation time: 20 minutes, plus 8 hours soaking

100g (3½oz) millet, soaked for 8 hours, or overnight

1 tsp coconut oil

¼ tsp ground cinnamon

¼ tsp ground ginger

¼ tsp ground turmeric

¼ tsp vanilla powder

225ml (8fl oz) coconut milk, plus extra if needed

235ml (8½fl oz) water

pinch of salt

Toppings

2–4 small figs, quartered

2 tbsp honey (optional)

handful of chopped pistachios (optional)

1 tsp hemp seeds

Rinse the millet in a fine-mesh strainer under running water and then drain.

Preheat the oven to 180°C (350°F), Gas Mark 4. Place the figs in an ovenproof dish and bake for 15 minutes until they are juicy and syrupy.

Heat the coconut oil in a small saucepan over a medium heat. Add the cinnamon, ginger, turmeric and vanilla and stir. When fragrant, after about 30 seconds, add the rinsed millet and a pinch of salt and stir to coat for 2–3 minutes, lightly toasting the millet.

Add the milk and water and stir. Bring to the boil, then reduce the heat, cover and simmer gently, stirring often to make sure it doesn't stick to the bottom of the saucepan. After about 15 minutes most of the liquid should have been absorbed and the porridge will have a thick and creamy consistency. If the mixture looks dry before the grains are tender, add a little more coconut milk.

Spoon into bowls and top each with figs, honey (if using), pistachios (if using) and hemp seeds.

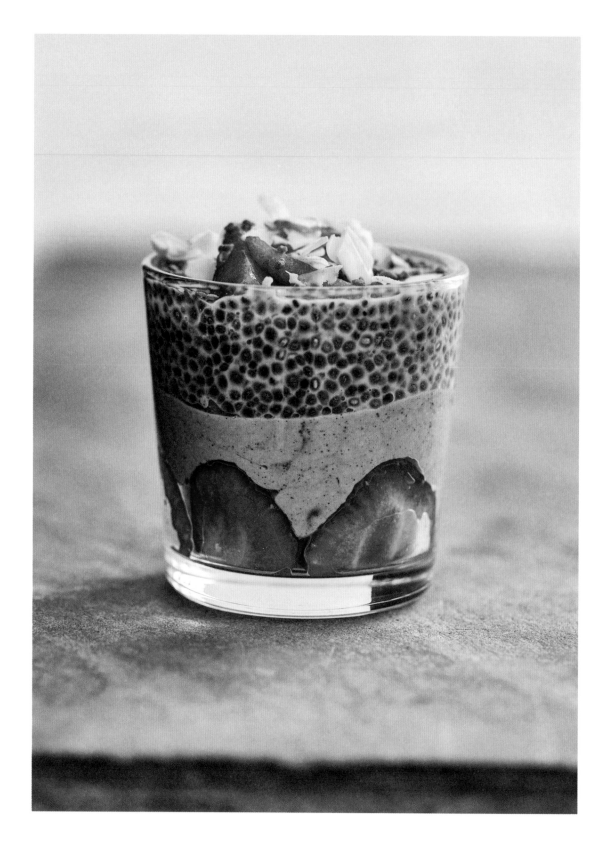

Probiotic Jar

This recipe will give you a beautiful probiotic parfait jar. We serve it at the restaurant and people always say how lovely this jar looks. Probiotic yogurt is full of good bacteria, which stabilize the gut, and the addition of spirulina makes it rich in minerals and protein. Chia is great for speeding up digestion, as well as being high in omega-3s. Enjoy taking care of your gut health with this beautiful jar of goodness.

Makes 4 x 250ml (9fl oz) jars
Preparation time: 25 minutes

For the chia pudding
475ml (17fl oz) homemade Nut & Seed Milk (*see* page 78)
1 tbsp honey or other sweetener (optional)
½ tsp vanilla extract
6 tbsp chia seeds

For the probiotic spirulina yogurt
500g Cashew Yogurt (*see* page 76)
¼ tsp vanilla powder
1 tbsp raw honey or other sweetener (optional)
½ tsp spirulina powder
pinch of salt

To serve
150g (5½oz) strawberries, sliced
2 tbsp bee pollen (optional)
25g (1oz) coconut chips
25g (1oz) flaked almonds

To make the chia pudding, blend the nut or seed milk with the honey (if using) and vanilla extract in a mixing bowl. Stir in the chia seeds until well combined. Soak until the seeds have absorbed all the liquid and become gelatinous. This mixture will keep for 3 days in a sealed container in the refrigerator.

To make the yogurt blend all the ingredients together in a high-speed blender until well combined.

To assemble, put a layer of strawberry slices around the edge of the base of the jars and add some yogurt. Spoon a layer of chia pudding on top of this. Finish with more strawberry slices, the bee pollen (if using), coconut chips and flaked almonds.

Protein Omelette

Serves 4
**Preparation time: 25 minutes, plus
    5 minutes cooking**

For the omelettes
375ml (13fl oz) water
190g (6½oz) chickpea flour
5 tbsp olive oil
¼ tsp salt
4 tbsp coconut oil, for frying

For the creamy harissa sauce
35g (1¼oz) carrots
1 red chilli
1 tbsp Farmacy Seed Mix
1 garlic clove, crushed
1 tbsp olive oil
50g (1¾oz) onion, chopped
175g (6oz) red pepper, chopped
50g (1¾oz) tomato, chopped
pinch of paprika

For the yogurt cream
150ml (¼ pint) Cashew Yogurt (*see* page 76)
2 tbsp nutritional yeast
salt and pepper

For the filling
2 tbsp olive oil
2 garlic cloves, finely chopped
400g (14oz) chard or stemmed spinach,
    leaves and stems separated

To serve
Roasted Red Pepper Confit (*see* page 208)
sprouts
coriander

A recipe inspired by socca *Niçoise* from the South of France. This delicate chickpea flour omelette is a fresh and healthy alternative to a traditional egg one and can be served with a combination of fillings. We add chard, a yogurt cream and a roasted carrot harissa sauce. Chickpeas and cashews are a great source of protein and provide a healthy start to your day.

Preheat the oven to 200°C (400°F), Gas Mark 6.

Prepare the omelettes by adding all the ingredients to a blender and blitz until combined. Transfer to a jug and set aside to rest for 15 minutes.

Meanwhile make the sauce. Place all the ingredients on a baking tray and roast in the oven for 25 minutes. Remove and allow to cool slightly before adding to a food processor. Blend until you have a smooth, creamy sauce.

While the vegetables for the sauce are roasting, make the yogurt cream by mixing all the ingredients in a bowl and set aside.

To make the omelettes, heat a small nonstick frying pan over a medium heat and add 1 tablespoon of coconut oil. Pour in enough batter to create a thin omelette about 15cm (6in) in diameter. Cook on one side until lightly browned and crisp, then flip and do the same on the other side. Place on a tray lined with greaseproof paper and repeat the process, putting a sheet of greaseproof paper between each omelette as you stack them up. These can be kept in a low oven while you make the filling.

For the filling, heat the olive oil in a large frying pan. Add the chard or spinach stems and sauté until softened, about 5 minutes, then add the leaves and continue until just wilted. Add the garlic and toss everything together for a further minute.

To serve, smear yogurt cream on an omelette, top with sautéed chard, a dollop of the sauce, Roasted Red Pepper Confit, a few sprouts and some coriander leaves.

Green Smoothie Bowl

GF NF R (if granola not used)
VG (if bee pollen not used)

This fresh, green and vibrant bowl will wake you up and help you start the day feeling energized and well-fuelled. It's a great way to consume a healthy hit of vitamins and minerals in the morning. The ingredients blend well together, allowing for optimum digestion and nutrition at the start of your day.

Serves 2–3
Preparation time: 10 minutes

3 peaches, pitted
½ banana
½ avocado
125g (4½oz) fresh spinach
300ml (½ pint) coconut water
10 mint leaves

To serve
Sprouted Quinoa Granola (*see* page 94)
bee pollen (optional)
fresh berries
mint leaves

Put all the ingredients in a blender and whizz until smooth and colourful.

Pour into bowls and decorate with granola (if using), bee pollen (if using), fresh berries and mint leaves.

Sprouted Quinoa Granola

This recipe offers you a delicious nut-free and grain-free seed granola bursting with nutrients and vitamins.

Serves 12

Preparation time: 10 minutes, plus soaking and sprouting, plus 40 minutes cooking

200ml (7fl oz) Homemade Apple Sauce (*see* opposite)

4 tbsp maple syrup

3 tbsp tahini

1 tsp vanilla extract

350g (12oz) sprouted quinoa (*see* page 53)

70g (2½oz) sunflower seeds

70g (2½oz) pumpkin seeds

2 tsp ground cinnamon

pinch of salt

30g (1oz) raisins

30g (1oz) goji berries

Preheat the oven to 150°C (300°F), Gas Mark 2. In a small bowl mix together the Apple Sauce, maple syrup, tahini and vanilla until you have a thick paste.

In a large mixing bowl, combine the quinoa, sunflower and pumpkin seeds, cinnamon and salt. Pour the apple sauce mixture over the quinoa and seeds and mix until well combined.

Spread the granola evenly over a baking tray lined with greaseproof paper and bake in the oven for 20 minutes. Remove the tray, stir the granola minimally to ensure you keep nice big clumps and bake for another 20 minutes, until toasted.

Allow the granola to cool, then add the raisins and goji berries. Store in an airtight container.

Homemade Apple Sauce

A healthy breakfast accompaniment for a tangy contrast of flavour, providing a good source of fibre, vitamin C, and loaded with plenty of beneficial antioxidants.

Quantity: 1 litres (1¾ pints)
**Preparation time: 10 minutes,
    plus 20 minutes cooking**

10 medium apples (most varieties
    will work but a sweet variety will
    eliminate the need to add sweetener),
    peeled, cored and sliced

235ml (8½fl oz) water

pinch of ground cinnamon (optional)

sweetener of choice (optional)

squeeze of lemon juice (optional)

Put the apple slices in a large saucepan, add the water and cover. Bring to the boil over a medium-high heat, then reduce the heat and simmer, stirring occasionally, until the apples break down into a thick sauce. This will take about 20 minutes.

Pour the cooked apple into a blender and whizz until smooth. Taste and add any of the optional ingredients to taste.

Store in a refrigerator for 1 week, or freeze.

Fluffy Pancakes

GF NF (if nut milk not used)
VG

Everyone loves pancakes and this recipe offers a healthy, gluten-free version of the family favourite. The buckwheat is a nourishing and energizing alternative to the flour traditionally used in pancake making. Buckwheat is non-allergenic and contains high levels of rutin, which helps combat high blood pressure, and there are plenty of easily digestible proteins here too. This is delicious as a breakfast dish or a dessert.

Serves 5
Preparation time: 25 minutes

50g (1¾oz) gluten-free oat flour (or whizz rolled oats in a blender to make flour)

100g (3½oz) buckwheat flour

200ml (7fl oz) unsweetened Homemade Apple Sauce (*see* page 95)

125ml (4fl oz) dairy-free milk

2 tbsp maple syrup

1 tsp baking powder

1 tsp baking soda

2 tsp lemon juice

1 tsp vanilla extract

To serve
sliced bananas
fresh berries
Chia Jam (*see* page 72)
coconut yogurt
maple syrup

Place all the ingredients in a blender and purée until smooth.

Heat a nonstick frying pan over a medium-high heat and, when hot, pour 150ml (¼ pint) of pancake batter into the centre of the pan and spread it in a circle with the back of a spoon, keeping it reasonably thick. Cook for 2–3 minutes.

Slide a spatula underneath the pancake, flip it over and cook for another 2–3 minutes before removing it from the pan. Put the pancake on a warm plate and cover with a tea towel. Repeat until you have used up all the batter.

Serve with banana slices, berries, jam, coconut yogurt and a drizzle of maple syrup.

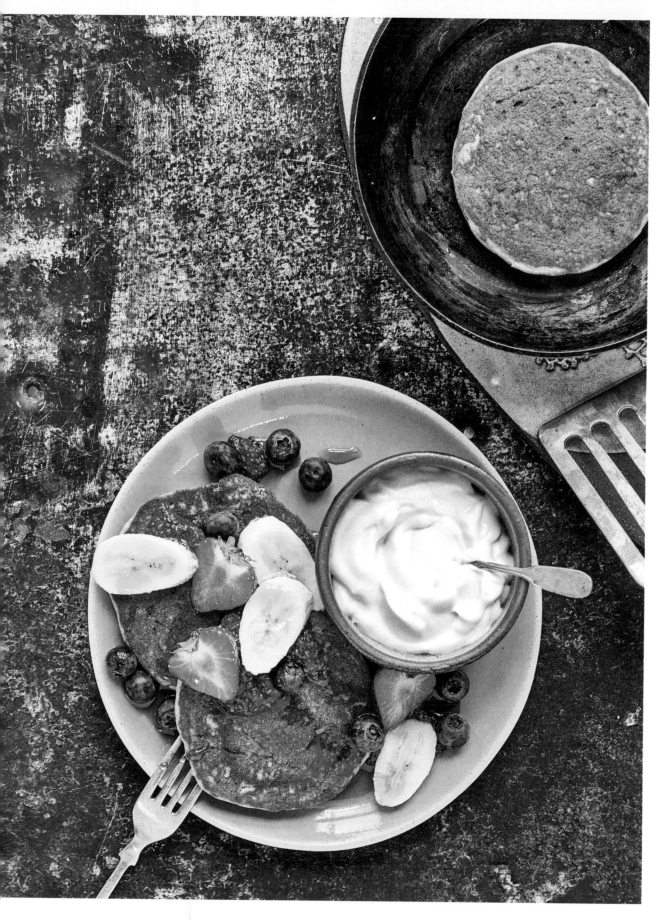

Seed Loaf with Farmacy Butter

This seedy loaf is highly nutritious and simple to make. We came up with this recipe when we wanted to make tasty bread that helps you feel energized after eating it. The loaf is flour-free and high in protein, as well as containing vitamins, minerals and good oils. It tastes great toasted and served with butter and Fruit Chia Jam (*see* page 72).

Serves 10 (makes 1 loaf; 10 slices)
**Preparation time: 10 minutes, plus
   6 hours refrigeration and 1 hour baking**

For the loaf
85g (3oz) teff flakes
85g (3oz) gluten-free rolled oats
85g (3oz) ground almonds
2 tbsp chia seeds
140g (5oz) sunflower seeds
85g (3oz) flaxseeds
3 tbsp psyllium husks
4 tbsp coconut oil
350ml (12fl oz) water
1 tbsp apple cider vinegar
1½ tbsp coconut nectar or other sweetener
1 tsp salt

For the butter
8 tbsp coconut oil
2 tbsp flaxseed oil
large pinch ground turmeric
pinch of salt

Line a 20cm (8in) loaf tin with greaseproof paper.

Mix all the dry loaf ingredients in a bowl. Add the wet ingredients and mix until well combined. Put the dough in the prepared tin.

Refrigerate for 6 hours, or overnight.

When you're ready to bake the loaf, preheat the oven to 150°C (300°F), Gas Mark 2. Bake the loaf for 1 hour, until brown. Push a narrow knife into the loaf; if it comes out dry, the loaf is cooked.

Make the butter by mixing or blending all the ingredients. Place the mixture in the refrigerator to set.

Serve slices of the loaf toasted and topped with the butter.

Breakfast Loaf

This banana breakfast loaf has a sweetness and texture that is great for the morning, and delicious topped with some Cashew Yogurt (*see* page 76). Or you could try eating it as a healthy treat in the afternoon with tea. Blueberries contain one of the highest antioxidant levels of any berry. They help to combat ageing, boost focus and memory and promote good skin condition. Bananas provide potassium, fibre and a range of vitamins. It's important to use ripe bananas for this recipe to give the loaf sweetness.

Serves 10 (makes 1 loaf; 10 slices)
Preparation time: 15 minutes,
plus 50 minutes baking

3 ripe bananas, plus 1 for the top (optional)

4 tbsp coconut oil, melted

5½ tbsp maple syrup

1 tbsp ground flaxseed mixed with 2½ tbsp water, and left for 5 minutes

1½ tsp vanilla extract

140g (5oz) gluten-free oat flour (or whizz rolled oats in a blender make flour)

70g (2½oz) ground almonds

1 tsp ground cinnamon

1 tsp gluten-free baking powder

½ tsp baking soda

pinch of salt

50g (1¾oz) walnuts, chopped, plus extra for decoration

50g (1¾oz) blueberries

Preheat the oven to 180°C (350°F), Gas Mark 4. Line a 20cm (8in) loaf tin with greaseproof paper.

In a food processor, mix together the bananas, coconut oil, maple syrup, flaxseed mixture and vanilla extract until well combined. Add the oat flour, ground almonds, cinnamon, baking powder, baking soda and salt and continue mixing until all are incorporated.

Fold in the chopped walnuts and blueberries, then pour the batter evenly into the prepared tin.

If using a fourth banana, slice it in half lengthways, and press it into the top of the loaf, cut side up, and sprinkle chopped walnuts around it. Lightly press the walnuts into the top.

Bake in the oven for 50–60 minutes or until a toothpick pushed into the loaf comes out clean. Allow the bread to cool on a cooling rack before slicing and eating.

We love dips and snacks at Farmacy. This is our collection of favourites to share with you. There are ideas for food on the run, dips to share with friends over drinks and delicious appetizers to serve before the main event.

Dips & Appetizers

Miso with Hemp Seeds

This dip uses a healthy brown miso without the harmful **GMO** that is in some other miso recipes. Enjoy the deep umami flavours of miso with healthy ingredients that support a strong immune system, healthy nervous system and bone health. The alkalizing nature of the ingredients keeps the body strong and helps to repel infections. Hemp seeds are added for crunch, a magical flavour and a further boost of good nutrients. This is a great, easy snack to serve any time. Try it with some freshly cut vegetable sticks.

Serves 8
Preparation time: 10 minutes

2 tbsp lemon juice
2 tbsp lime juice
2 garlic cloves, crushed
3 tbsp brown rice miso
2 tbsp tahini
1 tsp sesame oil
125ml (4fl oz) Seaweed Broth (*see* page 61)
1 tsp coconut nectar

To serve
cucumber sticks
carrot sticks
hemp seeds

Infuse the lemon and lime juice with the garlic for 10 minutes and then strain and discard the garlic.

Place the infused lemon and lime juice, miso, tahini, sesame oil, broth and coconut nectar in a food processor and whizz until it has a soft consistency similar to mayonnaise. Refrigerate overnight to allow the flavours to develop.

Just before serving, dry toast the hemp seeds. Mix them into the dip and serve with crudités.

Store in an airtight container in the refrigerator for up to 2 weeks.

Mayan Dip with Lime

The inspiration for this dip is an ancient Mayan recipe. It is updated here with a twist, including sun-dried tomatoes and rocket for a fresh, lively taste and a big flavour. The Mayans ate a lot of pumpkin seeds, which provide essential levels of magnesium, zinc and omega-3 fats. This seed dip is loaded with goodness and essential elements.

Serves 6
Preparation time: 15 minutes

125g (4½oz) pumpkin seeds
4 tbsp olive oil
1 onion, finely chopped
1 garlic clove, minced
100g (3½oz) chopped rocket
1 green chilli, whole
25g (1oz) chopped coriander
zest of 1 lime
2 tbsp lime juice
1 tbsp extra-virgin olive oil
½ tomato, cored and seeded
70g (2½oz) sun-dried tomatoes
60ml (4 tbsp) Vegetable Broth (*see* page 60)
salt

Toast the pumpkin seeds in 1 tablespoon of the olive oil. Sprinkle salt over them and set them aside.

In a frying pan gently sauté the onion, garlic and chilli in the remaining olive oil until the onion is translucent. Transfer to a food processor along with the rest of the ingredients. Process for about 4 minutes or longer for a smoother texture.

Tip into a serving bowl and serve.

Store in an airtight container in the refrigerator for up to 3 days.

Pictured overleaf, from left to right:
Mayan Dip with Lime, Farmacy Hummus,
Miso with Hemp Seeds, Spicy Queso

Spicy Queso

The Farmacy kitchen takes on the iconic nacho cheese dip in this fun dish full of healthy ingredients. Aubergines are a great source of dietary fibre, vitamins and minerals, including manganese, copper, iron and potassium.
The dish is rich in antioxidants and supports cardiovascular health as well as protecting from free radicals. It tastes pretty good too!
This is a dish to share with friends alongside a bowl of crunchy nachos. It's also easy to make a nut-free version – just take out the cashews and you're good to go.

Serves 8

Preparation time: 5 minutes, plus 1 hour salting and 30 minutes cooking and cooling

1 medium aubergine, cut into 1cm (½in) slices and salted for 1 hour

325ml (11fl oz) almond milk (or other dairy-free milk)

1 garlic clove

35g (1¼oz) cashews

2 red chillies

1 tsp Farmacy Seed Mix (*see* page 80)

4 tbsp nutritional yeast

½ medium tomato, seeded and chopped

2 tsp tapioca flour

4 tbsp olive oil

1 tsp smoked paprika

2 tbsp apple cider vinegar

Preheat the oven to 220°C (425°F), Gas Mark 7. Wipe the salted aubergine slices with clean kitchen paper, place on a nonstick baking tray and bake until just turning brown. This usually takes about 20 minutes.

Place the slices in a blender with all the other ingredients and blend until smooth and a thick creamy texture.

This can be stored in the refrigerator for up to 1 week.

Farmacy Hummus

Hummus is a firm favourite in our kitchen. There are many good recipes, but we love this one because it's so velvety, luxurious and tasty and is packed full of nutrients. This recipe is inspired by the exceptional version of hummus created at the Zahav Israeli restaurant and we think it delivers on flavour and nourishment. The garlic is infused during the process and then removed, rather than being left in the final mixture. As a result, the hummus has a softer flavour and lasts longer. Mixed with its own cooking broth, the hummus retains all the nutrients from the chickpeas. The addition of spirulina gives it an extra burst of nutrient-rich greens and colour. Make plenty; it will be eaten fast!

This recipe uses the chickpea broth before it is thickened and turned into aquafaba (*see* page 56). It's best to use dried chickpeas here. However, if you only have chickpeas from a jar, mix the aquafaba with an equal quantity of Vegetable Broth (*see* page 60) and use in place of the chickpea water in this recipe.

Serves 6
Preparation time: 5 minutes

4 garlic cloves, unpeeled
75ml (5 tbsp) lemon juice, plus extra to taste
1 tsp spirulina (optional)
1 tsp salt
6 tbsp tahini
320g (11oz) cooked chickpeas (*see* page 57), 125ml (4fl oz) cooking water reserved
½ tsp Farmacy Seed Mix (*see* page 80)
pinch of ground cumin (optional)
paprika and extra-virgin olive oil, to serve

Put the garlic, lemon juice, spirulina (if using) and salt in a food processor, whizz and then allow to sit for 10 minutes so the garlic mellows.

Strain the mixture through a fine-mesh sieve into a small bowl, pressing on the solids to release as much liquid as possible. Discard the solids.

Return the liquid to the food processor, add the tahini and pulse to combine. With the motor running, add the chickpea water a little at a time until the mixture is very smooth.

Add the cooked chickpeas and seed mix and process until smooth. Adjust the seasoning with salt, lemon juice and cumin, if using.

To serve, spoon the hummus into a shallow bowl, dust with paprika and drizzle generously with extra-virgin olive oil.

Store in an airtight container in the refrigerator for up to 4 days.

Goji Ketchup

This is a distinctive and colourful ketchup that you can use whenever you want a healthy sauce with a burst of flavour to add to your food. Goji berries contain a high dose of antioxidants and are a good source of protein and vitamin C. This delicious condiment has a load of nutrients that support healthy skin, too. A perfect accompaniment for our Baked Chickpea Sticks (*see* page 198).

Quantity: 8
**Preparation time: 5 minutes,
    plus 20 minutes soaking**

40g (1½oz) goji berries

20g (½oz) sun-dried tomatoes, halved

400g (14oz) can whole, peeled tomatoes

3 tsp apple cider vinegar

6 tsp maple syrup

2 tsp lemon juice

¼ tsp onion powder

1 tsp olive oil

½ tsp salt

pinch of pepper

Soak the goji berries and sun-dried tomatoes in a bowl of water for 20 minutes. Strain and discard the soaking water. Drain the canned tomatoes and discard the liquid.

Blend all the ingredients together in a food processor. Taste and add further seasoning to taste.

Keep in an airtight container in the refrigerator for up to 1 month.

Alioli

This is our no-egg version of alioli. The liquid from cooking chickpeas, called aquafaba (*see* page 56), replaces eggs and adds nutrients. When we give this lush and creamy dip to friends, they can't spot the difference between this and regular alioli – which we take as a big compliment.

We always think it's best to use aquafaba from cooking fresh, dried chickpeas, however we make an exception here and recommend using the liquid from jarred chickpeas as it emulsifies better.

Serves 4
Preparation time: 5 minutes

2 tbsp aquafaba (*see* page 56)
1 tbsp Dijon mustard
1 garlic clove
250ml (9fl oz) safflower or sunflower oil
2 tbsp lemon juice
salt

Place the aquafaba, mustard and garlic in a food processor and process at medium-high speed for 10 seconds.

Clean the sides of the food processor and set at medium speed, using the setting for mayonnaise if your machine has one.

Slowly add the oil in the thinnest possible stream; this will take about 4 minutes. It is important to add the oil very slowly as you need to allow the aquafaba to emulsify. Then add the lemon juice and salt to taste and serve.

Store in an airtight container in the refrigerator for 3–4 days.

Satay Sauce

A healthy and easy version of a classic Thai-inspired satay sauce. This is a quick and nourishing way to dress up roasted vegetables, eat with chickpea sticks, add to a stir-fry or use as a delicious topping on noodles. Peanuts are a great source of protein, biotin and a range of minerals. This sauce will give you a quick, no-stress burst of flavour which will be a great addition to your favourite supper.

Serves 6
Preparation time: 10 minutes

140g (5oz) unsalted peanuts

125ml (4fl oz) Vegetable Broth (*see* page 60), plus extra if required

2 garlic cloves, minced

½ tsp tamari

2 tsp sesame oil

1–2 tbsp coconut nectar

2 tbsp Alchemist's Sauce (*see* page 70)

2 tbsp lime juice

1 long red Thai chilli (or any type of chilli you have to hand), or more to taste

80ml (3fl oz) coconut milk

Toast the peanuts in a dry frying pan over a medium heat until lightly toasted.

Place the nuts and all the other ingredients in a food processor. Blend until they are well combined, adjusting the flavour as desired.

The sauce thickens on its own. If you are making this ahead of time and it becomes a little too thick, mix in a little extra broth before serving.

Store in an airtight container in the refrigerator for 3–4 days, or freeze.

Sweet Potato Cakes with Almond Butter Sauce

GF VG

These delicious sweet potato cakes are a firm favourite and one of our best-sellers in the restaurant. This is a quick and easy recipe loaded with protein and fibre and packed full of vitamins and minerals, including vitamins A and C and potassium. These little potato cakes make great finger food to snack on during the day, or to enjoy sharing as a starter. Ideal for picnics and lunchboxes, too.

Serves 4
**Preparation time: 20 minutes,
  plus cooking quinoa**

For the potato cakes
250g (9oz) sweet potato, peeled and cut
  into large cubes
100g (3½oz) quinoa, soaked (*see* page 51)
2 tbsp lemon juice
handful of fresh parsley, finely chopped
½ tsp paprika
pinch of salt and pepper
30g (1oz) brown rice flour
75g (2½oz) sesame seeds
coconut oil for frying

For the almond butter sauce
2 tbsp almond butter
1 tbsp Dijon mustard
1½ tbsp lemon juice
125–200ml (4–7fl oz) water

To serve
Green Sauce (*see* page 66), optional

Put the sweet potatoes into a saucepan of boiling water and cook until they are soft enough to break with a fork.

Cook the quinoa (*see* page 5), allow it to cool and set aside. (We use a rice cooker to do this; if you do this add 200ml (7fl oz) of liquid per 185g (6½oz) of quinoa.)

In a large bowl mix together all the ingredients except the rice flour and sesame seeds. Shape the mixture into rounds (this recipe will yield about 16 to 20 cakes), using the rice flour to shape them and create a non-stick coating. Dredge in the sesame seeds and chill in the refrigerator to set for a couple of hours.

When set, cook the potato cakes in coconut oil in a frying pan over a medium-low heat until golden brown and a little crisp on both sides.

To make the almond butter sauce, combine all the ingredients in bowl and mix until smooth.

Serve with the potato cakes and drizzle a little Green Sauce over the top, if liked.

DIPS & APPETIZERS 119

Aubergine Rolls with Green Sauce

Serves 8
Preparation time: 45 minutes,
   plus 2 hours soaking

For the aubergine rolls
2 large, pear-shaped aubergines, cut
   lengthways into 1cm (½in) slices
salt
olive oil

For the sunflower seed pâté
140g (5oz) sunflower seeds, soaked for
   2 hours, then drained
4 tbsp Vegetable Broth (*see* page 60),
   plus extra if needed
2 tbsp tahini
4–5 tbsp lemon juice
1 tsp apple cider vinegar
pinch of nutmeg
4 basil leaves
chilli flakes (optional)
salt and pepper, to taste

For the lettuce filling
50g (1¾oz) lamb's lettuce or rocket leaves
1½ tbsp lemon juice
1½ tbsp olive oil

To garnish
Green Sauce (*see* page 66)

This is our plant-based version of a sushi roll. Choose the pear-shaped variety of aubergine for this dish as they are a better shape for rolling. This recipe is a great source of essential fatty acids, providing plenty of protein, is nut-free, easy to digest and full of flavour. Beautiful nourishing finger food that looks gorgeous on the plate.

Lay the aubergine slices on a plate and salt them for about 1 hour until the water has seeped out of them.

Preheat the oven to 220°C (475°F), Gas Mark 9.

Wipe the slices dry with kitchen paper and place on a non-stick baking tray. Bake in the oven for 5–7 minutes, turning once, until the slices start going brown. They should be golden and cooked through, but not mushy. Handle them with care; they will be the outer wrapping of the sushi.

To make the sunflower seed pâté, put the ingredients in a blender and blitz at high speed until they become a creamy, spreadable mixture. If the mixture is too dry, add more vegetable broth until you have the right texture.

Sprinkle the lamb's lettuce or rocket leaves with lemon juice, salt and a little olive oil.

To assemble the rolls, spread a thin layer of pâté along the length of an aubergine slice. Take a few leaves and place them at the narrower end of the slice. Start rolling from this end towards the wider end.

Repeat with all the aubergine slices, then place them on a plate seam side down so that the leaves come out of both ends. Top the aubergine rolls with a drizzle of green sauce. Serve at room temperature or deliciously cold.

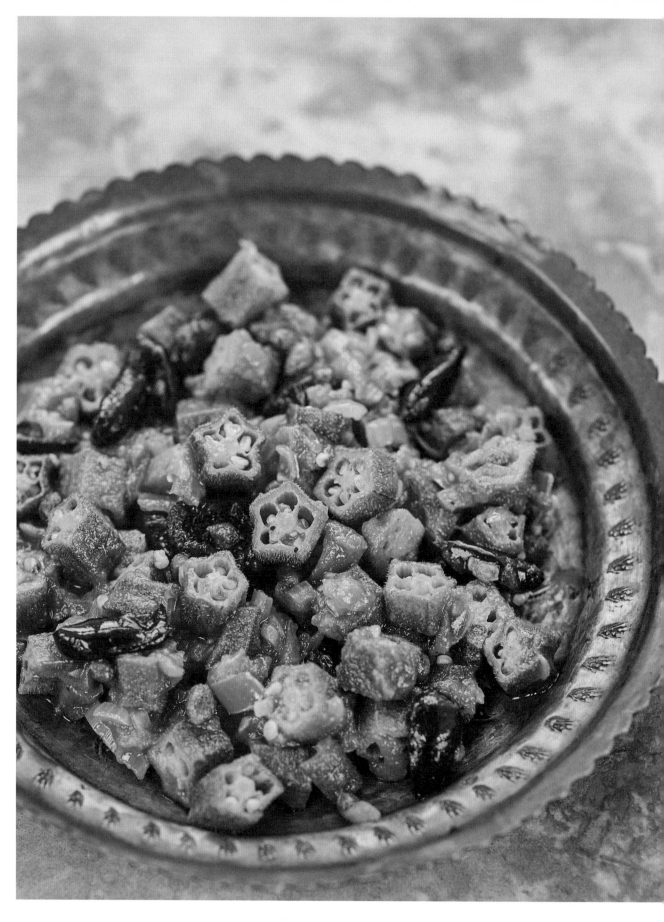

Okra Caponata

Inspired by the Sicilian classic recipe, this dish replaces aubergine with okra and adds some flavours that take it to new heights. Okra is rich in vitamins and minerals and supplies healthy doses of calcium, iron, magnesium, potassium and zinc. It's great for fibre, too. The turmeric has bioactive compounds with powerful medicinal properties, and is anti-inflammatory and high in antioxidants. Great served hot, cold or at room temperature, this tastes even better the next day.

Serves 6
**Preparation time: 10 minutes,
  plus 16 minutes cooking**

½ onion, chopped

1 celery stick, leaves attached, chopped

2 tbsp coconut oil

500g (1lb 2oz) okra, chopped into
  1cm (½in) slices

1 tsp ground turmeric

1 garlic clove, chopped

300g (10½oz) fresh tomatoes, chopped

1 tbsp capers

8 black olives, pitted and halved

2 tbsp apple cider vinegar

2 tsp coconut nectar

salt

Place the onion and the celery in a saucepan with 1 tablespoon of the coconut oil and sauté over a low heat until translucent. Add the okra and another tablespoon of coconut oil and sauté for 6–8 minutes.

Add the turmeric and garlic and sauté for a further minute. Add the tomatoes, stir and cover the saucepan. Reduce the heat to very low and cook for 6 minutes, or until the okra is tender.

Remove from the heat and add the capers, olives, vinegar and coconut nectar. Stir and check the seasoning. This dish can be served hot, at room temperature or refrigerator cold.

Cauliflower Nuggets

These cauliflower nuggets have the wonderfully crunchy texture that is usually the result of breading and frying. Fun to eat and great to share, try them as a quick eat-and-go snack, or serve with drinks as a pre-dinner nibble with friends.

Serves 6

Preparation time: 25 minutes, plus 30 minutes baking

1 medium head cauliflower, cored and cut into bite-sized florets

1 tsp Philosopher's Sauce (*see* page 64)

4 tbsp lime juice

100g (3½oz) gluten-free rolled oats

45g (1½oz) desiccated coconut

1 red chilli

1 tsp fine salt

1 tsp smoked paprika

¼ tsp pepper

75g (2¾oz) hemp seeds

75g (2¾oz) linseeds

75g (2¾oz) poppy seeds

75g (2¾oz) black sesame seeds

125g (4½oz) almond butter

1 tbsp lemon juice

small handful of coriander, chopped

Preheat the oven to 200°C (400°F), Gas Mark 6. Line a large baking sheet with greaseproof paper.

Mix the cauliflower florets in the Philosopher's sauce and lime juice and set aside to marinate for about 20 minutes.

In a food processor, blend the oats, coconut, chilli, salt, paprika and black pepper until they have a mealy texture. Do not over-process or make the texture too fine; you need a coarse texture.

Add all the seeds, stir and transfer the mixture to a shallow bowl for dredging.

Thin the almond butter with 4 tablespoons of water and the lemon juice to create a batter. If it's too thick, add a little more water to give you a creamy texture.

Dip the florets into the batter, dredge in the oatmeal and seed coating and place on a baking tray.

Bake in the oven for 30 minutes. Remove from the oven, sprinkle with the chopped coriander and serve in a beautiful bowl.

Wild Teff Wraps with Mushroom Filling

Serves 6
Preparation time: 20 minutes,
**   plus 5 minutes cooking**

For the wraps
125g (4½oz) teff flour
275ml (9fl oz) water
½ tsp ground turmeric
½ tsp cracked peppercorns
salt
olive oil, for frying

For the sprout salad
35g (1¼oz) lentil sprouts (*see* page 53)
35g (1¼oz) fenugreek sprouts (*see* page 53)
75ml (5 tbsp) olive oil
75ml (5 tbsp) lemon juice
¼ tsp salt
¼ tsp coconut nectar

For the mushrooms
100g (3½oz) shiitake mushrooms, sliced
2 tbsp sesame oil
1 garlic clove, grated
1 tsp Philosopher's Sauce (*see* page 64)
2 tbsp lime juice
salt

To serve
Satay Sauce (*see* page 117)
85g (3oz) rocket, chopped, salted and
    lightly oiled
10g (¼oz) toasted pumpkin seeds

Teff is one of the smallest grains in the world, similar in size to a poppy seed. It's the most nutritious of all the grains, with a high fibre content and is a great source of protein, manganese, iron and calcium. Teff also acts as a probiotic. This healthy wrap is served with nutritious sprouts – light to eat and very tasty.

Mix together all the ingredients for the wraps. This batter may seem a little watery, but that is intentional. Set aside.

Make the salad by mixing the sprouts together. Put the rest of the ingredients into a screw-top jar and mix by shaking it vigorously. Pour over the sprouts and set aside.

Sauté the mushrooms in the sesame oil in a frying pan over a high heat. When seared on one side, add the garlic, Philosopher's Sauce, lime juice and salt, stir, remove from the heat and put into a dish.

Make the wraps in a nonstick, heavy-based frying pan. Add enough oil to just cover the base of the pan. Pour 2 tablespoons of batter into the centre of the pan, let it spread out so the wrap is as thin as possible and holds its shape and cook until the top is no longer wet and the wrap has a lacy appearance. Carefully flip it and cook for a further minute. Aim for a wrap size of 8–10cm (3¼–4in). You may have to test one or two to get the right cooking temperature. Repeat until you have used up all the batter.

To assemble, take a wrap and spread it with Satay Sauce. Top with rocket, sprout salad, mushrooms and some toasted pumpkin seeds.

Note

Use a good-quality frying pan made of non-toxic material that cooks well at high temperatures to prevent the wraps sticking. The Kitchen Equipment section (*see* page 46–8) gives more information on pans.

Chickpea Popcorn

This crunchy, spicy take on popcorn is perfect for party nibbles, movie snacks, taking to the beach or adding to a lunchbox and adds high levels of fibre, protein, iron and zinc to your diet. Choose small chickpeas for this recipe and be sure to make plenty. Ideal for sharing.

Serves 4
Preparation time: 5 minutes

500g (1lb 2oz) cooked chickpeas
  (the smallest you can find)
2 tbsp olive oil
1½ tsp Farmacy Seed Mix (*see* page 80)
1 tsp smoked paprika
½ tsp salt

Preheat the oven to 180°C (400°F), Gas Mark 6.

Put all the ingredients in a large bowl and toss until the chickpeas are well coated.

Place on a baking tray and bake in the middle of the oven until crisp. This usually takes about 50 minutes.

Soups are a perfect way to get a hit of nutrients with maximum taste and versatility. Each soup in this collection is a special combination with a unique taste. Easy to make in advance to keep eating well as part of a busy lifestyle. The salads give a powerful punch of taste, colour, nutrition and vibrancy. Food that is good to eat anytime, across the seasons.

Soups & Salads

Farm Green Soup

This soup is a Farmacy classic that has a wonderful depth of taste and delivers fibre, healthy fats, protein and a range of vitamins in one delicious bowl of goodness. The watercress contains vitamin C, more calcium than milk, more iron than spinach and more folate than bananas. In the winter, serve the soup warm with a dash of olive oil. In the summer, serve it cold with a spoonful of Farmacy Cashew Yogurt.

Serves 4
Preparation time: 15–20 minutes, plus soaking time

1 tbsp cold-pressed coconut oil

1 leek, chopped

2 garlic cloves, chopped

1 large head of broccoli, cut into bite-sized pieces, stem peeled and chopped

850ml (1½ pints) Vegetable Broth (*see* page 60), plus extra if needed

1 tsp salt

200g (7oz) Swiss chard, stems removed (keep the stems for Mushrooms and Chard Stems with Tarragon Sauce – *see* page 190)

100g (3½oz) watercress

1 tsp spirulina

½ very ripe avocado

1½ tbsp lemon juice

35g (1¼oz) almonds, soaked (optional, *see* page 49)

To garnish
toasted pumpkin seeds
sprouts
Cashew Yogurt (*see* page 76)
olive oil, to drizzle

Put the coconut oil into a heavy-based saucepan over a medium heat and sauté the leek until soft. Add the garlic and sauté for a further minute.

Add the broccoli, broth and salt and bring to the boil. Reduce the heat and simmer for 5 minutes. Add the chard and cook for a further 5 minutes.

Remove the pan from the heat and stir in the watercress and spirulina. Let the soup cool slightly, then transfer to a blender with the avocado, lemon juice and soaked almonds, if using. Blend until smooth. The longer it's processed, the smoother the soup will become. If it's too thick, add more stock until it becomes creamy.

Garnish with toasted pumpkin seeds, sprouts, Cashew Yogurt and a swirl of olive oil.

132 SOUPS & SALADS

Celestial Purple Soup

This is one of Camilla's special recipes that she loves to make for friends; a simple soup that is a beautiful colour. Cauliflower is one of the most nutritious of the cruciferous vegetables and is high in vitamin C and other vitamins and minerals. It's anti-inflammatory, detoxifying, antioxidant-rich and a booster for brain and heart health. This stunning soup is ideal served as a delicious lunch or starter.

Serves 8

Preparation time: 4 minutes, plus 25 minutes cooking and 2 minutes blending

125g (4½oz) leeks, coarsely chopped

1 tbsp olive oil, plus extra for garnish

125g (4½oz) cauliflower florets

1 litre (1¾ pints) Vegetable Broth (*see* page 60)

600g (1lb 5oz) red cabbage, sliced

35g (1¼oz) almonds, soaked overnight (*see* page 49)

125ml (4fl oz) almond milk

salt

To garnish

Cashew Yogurt (*see* page 76)

beet sprouts

In a heavy-based saucepan, sauté the leeks in the olive oil for about 3 minutes until soft. Add the cauliflower and 125ml (4fl oz) of broth to the pan and cook until the cauliflower is almost cooked through; about 10 minutes.

Add the red cabbage and stir, making sure it is coated with the liquid. Cook for about 5 minutes, then reduce the heat to medium and add the rest of the stock. Turn off the heat and allow to steep for 20 minutes until cooled.

Put the mixture into a food processor with the drained almonds and almond milk and blend until very smooth.

Garnish with a swirl of olive oil, some cashew yogurt and a scattering of beet sprouts.

Kitchari Soup

This is a deeply nourishing soup fortified with sprouts, kale and turmeric. The combination creates a taste sensation. The sprouts in this dish are high in life-force energy and are anti-inflammatory, while the turmeric and nutrient-dense kale are loaded with antioxidants. This is delicious in any season and can be served hot or cold. We know we shouldn't have favourites, but we do. This is one of them.

Serves 6

Preparation time: 40 minutes, plus sprouting time

3 tbsp olive oil

½ onion, chopped

25g (1oz) chopped celery

small handful of coriander stems, finely chopped

2 garlic cloves, finely chopped

2 tsp Farmacy Seed Mix (*see* page 80)

1 tsp ground turmeric

125g (4½oz) kale, chopped

625ml (1 pint) Vegetable Broth (*see* page 60) or water

200g (7oz) sprouted mung beans (*see* page 53)

300ml (½ pint) coconut milk

100g (3½oz) tomatoes, seeded and chopped

2 tbsp coconut nectar

2 tbsp Philosopher's Sauce (*see* page 64)

salt and pepper

coriander leaves, to garnish

In a large saucepan, heat the olive oil and add the onion, celery and coriander stems. Cook for 3 minutes.

Add the garlic, seed mix and turmeric and cook for another minute. Add the kale with 125ml (4fl oz) of the broth or water and simmer for 5 minutes.

Next, add the mung beans, the rest of the broth, salt and pepper and stir well to combine. Cook until the beans are almost tender, about 10 minutes.

Add the coconut milk, tomatoes, coconut nectar and Philosopher's Sauce and simmer for another 10 minutes.

When the beans are ready, taste and adjust the salt as needed.

Garnish with the coriander leaves.

Note

This soup is like a stew and has a chunky texture. Be careful to avoid adding too much liquid.

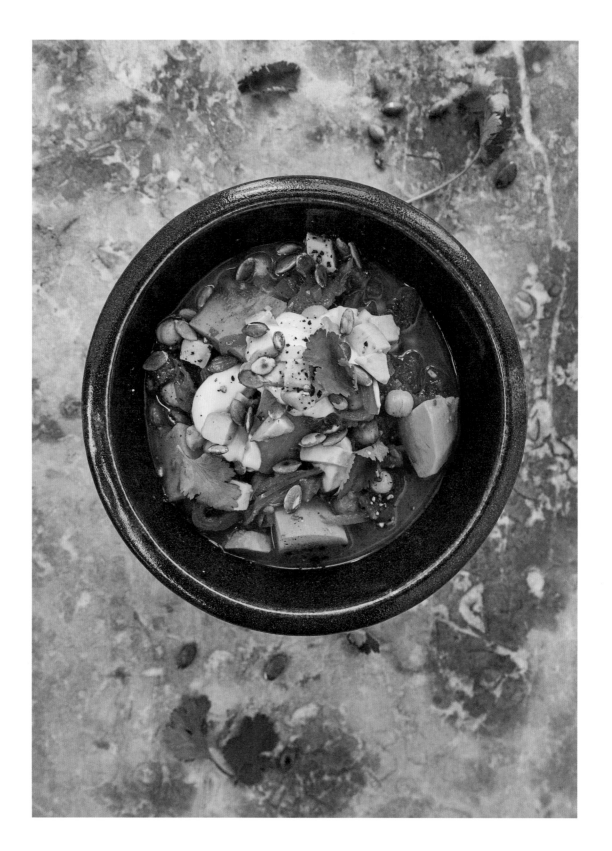

Mexican Soup

Serves 6–8
Preparation time: 30 minutes

1 tbsp coconut oil
½ red onion, diced
6 coriander sprigs, stems chopped, leaves to garnish
1 red pepper, thinly sliced
50g (1¾oz) celery tops, chopped
3 garlic cloves, finely chopped
1½ tbsp paprika (sweet or smoked)
1 tbsp ground cumin
2 tsp chopped oregano leaves
200g (7oz) tomatoes, chopped
1–2 red chillies, finely chopped (optional)
700ml (1¼ pints) Vegetable Broth (*see* page 60)
1 sweet potato, about 500g (1lb 2oz), diced
160g (5¾oz) cooked chickpeas
2–3 tbsp coconut nectar
4 tbsp lime juice
salt

To garnish
cubed avocado
toasted pumpkin seeds
roasted tomato skins, chopped (*see* page 140), optional
coconut yogurt

This hearty soup is perfect for getting cosy on cold days. It is inspired by an Aztec recipe called *pozole*. This is traditionally a ceremonial stew flavoured with a combination of New World foods such as smoked paprika, tomatoes and sweet peppers from Mexico and the Inca sweet potato. This version includes celery leaves, rich in vitamin E and calcium, and a variety of vegetables and spices that deliver vitamins and minerals. The coriander stems and leaves support toxic metal cleansing. A warm, nourishing dish with a deep flavour.

In a heavy-based saucepan heat the coconut oil over a medium-high heat and add the onion, coriander stems and pepper. Sauté for about 5 minutes until translucent and soft. Add the celery tops and garlic and sauté for 1 minute.

Add the paprika (use smoked for a deeper flavour) and the cumin and cook with the vegetables for 1–2 minutes, taking care not to burn the spices.

Add the oregano with the tomatoes and the chillies (if using) and cook for another 5 minutes, stirring regularly, until you have a deep red vegetable base. Add 450ml (16fl oz) of the broth, reserving 250ml (9fl oz) for later. Bring to the boil.

Add the sweet potato and simmer for 10 minutes, until it is soft but not mushy.

Add the chickpeas and coconut nectar and cook for 2 more minutes. Season with salt, remove from the heat and cover. The soup will be a chunky broth at this stage. Add some of the reserved broth if more liquid is needed and adjust the seasoning.

Before serving, add the lime juice. Garnish with avocado cubes, toasted pumpkin seeds, chopped tomato skins, coriander leaves and coconut yogurt.

Roasted Tomato Soup

This is one of Pietro's favourite recipes that he created with ingredients fresh from the garden – a classic tomato soup with a Farmacy twist designed to extract as much flavour as possible from the tomatoes. Tomatoes are one of nature's great umami offerings and roasting them intensifies the flavour. The challenge is to make a tomato soup that doesn't taste like tomato sauce. We've mixed it up and added some favourite ingredients to create a big-flavour, classic recipe. The tomato skins are used as they contain nutritional gems and this adds to the deep flavour of the soup. Serve cold gazpacho style, or warm with a spoonful of Farmacy Cashew Yogurt.

Serves 4

Preparation time: 5 minutes,
   plus 4 hours roasting

12 medium tomatoes, halved

3 tbsp nutritional yeast

2 tbsp cashews

2 black garlic cloves, left whole

4½ tbsp almond milk

1 tbsp Alchemist's Sauce (*see* page 70)

500ml (18fl oz) Vegetable Broth (*see* page 60)

To garnish

sprouts or microgreens

Cashew Yogurt (*see* page 76)

olive oil, for drizzling

Preheat the oven to 120°C (250°F), Gas Mark ½. Place the tomato halves cut side -down on a baking tray lined with greaseproof paper. Roast in the oven for 2 hours.

Remove the baking tray from the oven, peel the tomatoes and place the skins on an ovenproof dish. Remove the greaseproof paper from the baking tray, turn the tomatoes to expose the cut sides and return them to the oven alongside the skins.

Roast for a further 2 hours, then remove from the oven and allow to cool.

Mince the tomato skins using a knife or blitz them in a small food processor until they become almost salt-like and set aside.

Place the tomato flesh in a food processor with the nutritional yeast, cashews, garlic, almond milk, Alchemist's Sauce and the broth and blend until very smooth.

Serve garnished with the tomato skins, sprouts or microgreens, Cashew Yogurt and a swirl of olive oil.

Note

If your tomatoes are not quite ripe enough, add 1 tablespoon of coconut nectar to bolster its sweetness.

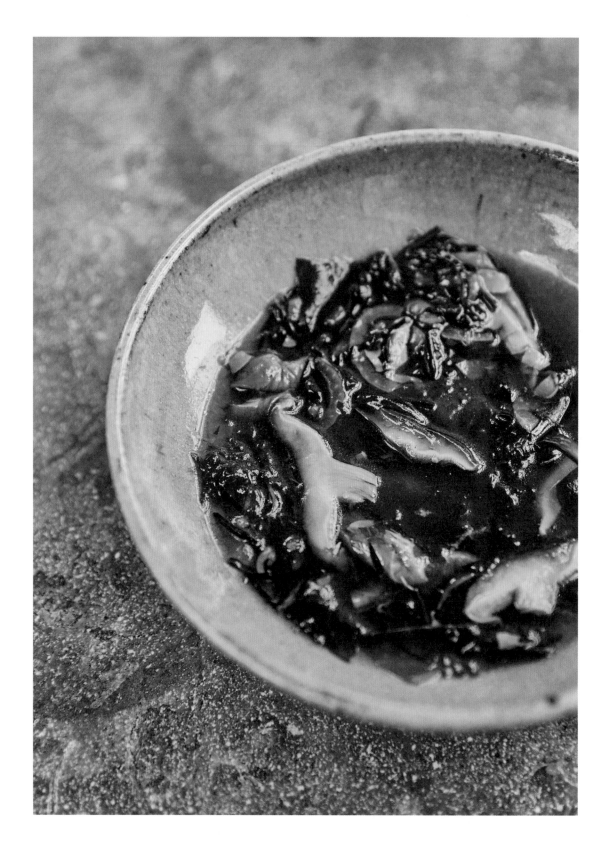

Sea Mineral & Mushroom Soup

The combination of seaweed and shiitake mushrooms in this dish gives you a strong boost of vitamins and minerals. There is so much goodness in every bowl. We would happily eat this every day.

Serves 6

Preparation time: 10 minutes, plus 10 minutes cooking

1 onion, thinly sliced

½ tbsp sesame oil

1 garlic clove, crushed

1 tbsp lime juice

1 tsp coconut nectar

300g (10½oz) fresh shiitake mushrooms, sliced

150g (5½oz) other mushrooms (eg chestnut, oyster, portobello), sliced

2 litres (3½ pints) warm water, or 1 litre (1¾ pints) Seaweed Broth (*see* page 61) and 1 litre (1¾ pints) Vegetable Broth (*see* page 60)

2 tbsp tamari

60g (2¼oz) dried mixed seaweed, soaked for 5 minutes

2 tbsp grated root ginger

1 tbsp rice vinegar

salt and freshly ground white pepper

In a heavy-based saucepan sauté the onion in the sesame oil until almost brown, being careful not to burn it.

Add the garlic and stir. Pour in half the lime juice and all the coconut nectar and mix. Add the mushrooms and a pinch of salt and sauté for about 4 minutes.

Add the water or broth, if using, along with the tamari. Bring to the boil, remove from the heat and add the seaweed, ginger and rice vinegar. Adjust the seasoning with salt, pepper and lime juice.

Serve in beautiful bowls.

Green Salad with Lentil Dressing

GF NF VG

This is a crowd pleaser that gets rave reviews whenever we serve it. Good for healthy fibre intake, this salad contains iron and supports the heart. We prefer not to use a lot of oil in our recipes and here we replace oil with a well-flavoured lentil sauce to create a protein-rich, nutritious salad. It's a simple dish to assemble, using ingredients already prepared from the Basics chapter (*see* page 58). The lentil dressing can be served cold in the summer or warm in winter and works as a healthy feast either way.

Serves 4
Preparation time: 10 minutes

1½ tbsp Dijon mustard
1 tbsp Farmacy Seed Mix (*see* page 80)
dash of tamari
1½ tbsp lemon juice
80ml (3fl oz) Vegetable Broth (*see* page 60)
175g (6oz) cooked green lentils (*see* page 57 for soaking and cooking)
1 crisp baby Romaine lettuce, or any sturdy greens
¼ tsp salt

To garnish
Roasted Red Pepper Confit (*see* page 208)
1 tbsp Farmacy Seed Mix (*see* page 80)
sprouts

Start by making the dressing. Mix together the mustard, seed mix, tamari and 1 tablespoon of lemon juice. If the dressing seems too thick, thin it by adding a little vegetable broth. Stir it into the cooked lentils.

Sprinkle the lettuce or greens with salt and a dash of lemon juice. Gently toss the leaves. Arrange them on a plate and top with the dressed lentils and roasted pepper strips. Garnish with the seed mix and sprouts.

Note

This dish works well using green lentils because they have a specific cooking time, a unique taste and a creamy consistency that is ideal here. We don't recommend using other types of lentils for this recipe.

Roasted Carrot & Avocado Salad

This salad includes the surprise combination of carrot and avocado. It's a mixture of flavours and textures that work so well together that it has become one of our favourite dishes to make for friends. Chia seeds are used to emulsify the dressing. This pretty, colourful salad is rich in fatty acids and vitamins and has an additional protein boost from the hazelnuts.

Serves 4
Preparation time: 10 minutes, plus 35 minutes roasting

12–16 baby carrots

1½ tbsp Farmacy Seed Mix (*see* page 80)

3 tbsp lime juice

3 tbsp olive oil

1 tsp sherry vinegar

1 red chilli

good pinch of salt

2 tsp chia seeds soaked in Seaweed Broth (*see* page 61)

400g (14oz) mixed rocket, mizuna and watercress leaves

1 ripe avocado, cubed

2 tbsp toasted and chopped hazelnuts

Preheat the oven to 200°C (400°F), Gas Mark 6. Rub the carrots with the seed mix and put in a roasting tin. Add 4 tablespoons of water, cover with greaseproof paper and roast in the oven for about 20 minutes.

Take the tin out of the oven, remove the greaseproof and return the carrots to the oven to roast for another 30 minutes until nicely caramelized. Remove from the oven and allow to cool.

Combine the lime juice, olive oil, sherry vinegar, whole chilli, pinch of salt and chia seeds. Whisk together for about a minute to create an emulsion, then set aside. Remove the chilli before serving.

In a serving bowl combine the leaves, carrots and avocado and toss with the emulsion. Serve topped with the hazelnuts.

Fennel & Spinach with Carrot Dressing

Here's a dish that captures the fresh flavours of the garden, combining spinach, fresh tomatoes and zingy fennel. It's packed full of vitamins and minerals, with good levels of fibre, zinc and calcium. The dressing is part of the family of dressings we create that use vegetables as a base. Here raw carrot combines with brown rice miso to create a silky, golden sauce. This recipe makes a perfect appetizer and can be doubled for more festive occasions and celebrations.

Serves 4
Preparation time: 15 minutes

For the salad
1 fennel bulb, thinly sliced
½ tsp salt
200g (7oz) baby spinach
20 cherry tomatoes, halved
toasted hemp seeds, to garnish

For the dressing
1 large carrot, roughly chopped
6 tbsp water
1½ tbsp brown rice miso
1 tbsp lime juice
1 tbsp white wine vinegar
4 tbsp sesame oil
2cm (¾in) piece of fresh root ginger
2 tbsp maple syrup

Rub the fennel slices with the salt and set aside for 5 minutes.

Make the dressing by putting all the ingredients into a food processor and blending until very smooth. Check for seasoning.

Arrange the salad on a serving plate, garnish with the toasted hemp seeds and serve with the dressing.

Beet Top Salad

This salad has a style of its own with its blend of intense colours. All parts of the beetroots are used including the leaves, which are highly perishable and therefore a great indicator of the freshness of the root. This salad tastes even better eaten the next day, as the flavours deepen. The dish is high in zinc and iron and contains protein, fibre, magnesium, potassium, copper and manganese. Beet greens also supply significant quantities of vitamin A and C, as well as calcium to help bone strength and support the immune system.

Serves 4–6

Preparation time: 20 minutes, plus 60 minutes roasting

3 beetroot (with green tops) plus extra beet tops (ask your greengrocer)

3 tbsp lemon juice

1 tbsp extra-virgin olive oil, plus extra for frying

1 garlic clove, crushed

2 tbsp tahini

1 tbsp apple cider vinegar

2 tsp coconut nectar

6 tbsp water

½ tsp brown rice miso

8 pencil-thin asparagus spears, or 8 thick spears cut diagonally

175g (6oz) cooked buckwheat (*see* page 51)

salt and pepper

To garnish

Cashew Yogurt (*see* page 76)

6 tbsp pomegranate seeds

35g (1¼oz) toasted pumpkin seeds

Preheat the oven to 200°C (400°F), Gas Mark 6.

Cut off the beet tops and set to one side. Place the beetroot on a baking tray lined with greaseproof paper and roast on the middle rack of the oven for about 1 hour.

Remove from the oven and, once the beetroot have cooled a little, peel the skins away with your hands. Cube the beetroot, dress with a dash of lemon juice and a drizzle of olive oil and set to one side.

To prepare the dressing, infuse the rest of the lemon juice with the crushed garlic and let it stand for 10 minutes. Strain and reserve the infused juice and discard the garlic. Blend together the infused lemon juice, the rest of the olive oil, the tahini, cider vinegar, coconut nectar, water and miso in a food processor.

Separate the beet leaves from the stems. Heat a frying pan over a high heat and sauté the leaves in olive oil for 30 seconds, then add salt and pepper and remove from the pan.

Cut the beet stems into 3cm (1¼in) pieces. Put them in the frying pan and sauté until almost charred. Sprinkle a little salt over them and taste. Once done, add the asparagus spears and cook until soft, about 5 minutes.

Combine the buckwheat, beet stems and asparagus, toss with two-thirds of the dressing and arrange on a serving plate. Toss the leaves with the remaining dressing and place on top of the buckwheat. Drizzle with the Cashew Yogurt, add the cubed beetroot and sprinkle with pomegranate and pumpkin seeds.

Note

The cubed beets will stain everything pink, so add at the end.

Kale & Sprouts with Almond Cream

This salad combines kale and sprouted beans. Kale is one of the great supergreens. It's high in fibre and packed with vitamins. The sprouted beans are full of natural, energy-giving life force and one of the most nutrient-dense sprouting foods. The kale is simmered, creating the perfect texture to mix with the beans. The lemon adds a tangy note which is a delicious contrast to the almond butter dressing. A great dish served warm on a cold day.

Serves 6
Preparation time: 10 minutes, plus 10 minutes cooking time

2 tsp olive oil

2 medium garlic cloves, minced

1 tbsp grated fresh root ginger

500g (1lb 2oz) elephant kale leaves, roughly chopped (avoid curlier kale)

125ml (4fl oz) Vegetable Broth (*see* page 60)

150g (5½oz) sprouted mung beans (*see* page 53)

1½ tbsp lemon juice, or to taste

2 tsp tamari, or to taste

For the dressing
2 tbsp almond butter

1½ tbsp lemon juice

½ tsp salt

4 tbsp water

Heat the olive oil in a heavy-based saucepan over a medium heat and briefly sauté the garlic and ginger.

Add the kale leaves and toss before adding the broth. Bring to the boil, reduce the heat and cover the pan. Simmer for 5 minutes.

Add the mung beans and simmer for another 5 minutes.

Add the lemon juice and tamari to taste. Add more lemon juice if necessary, then let the kale and mung beans rest off the heat for a couple of minutes.

For the dressing, mix the almond butter, lemon juice and salt in a bowl and slowly add the water. The consistency should be thick and creamy – not runny, but not too stiff either.

Spoon a tablespoon of the dressing on to a serving plate and spread it out to create a thin layer. Pile the kale and mung beans on top.

Note

Do not use unsprouted mung beans, as they will need to cook for 40 minutes, by which time the kale will be overcooked.

Sea Vegetable Salad

GF NF R VG

Serves 4
Preparation time: 30 minutes

For the cucumber marinade
5 tbsp rice vinegar
1 tbsp finely chopped dill
¾ tsp salt
¾ tsp coconut nectar

For the salad
1 large, seedless cucumber, thinly sliced
1 small carrot, sliced into matchsticks
½ tsp salt
85g (3oz) dried green mixed seaweed
60g (2¼oz) daikon radish, thinly sliced
1 small bunch of watercress
1 lime
2 tbsp dry toasted black sesame seeds
1 nori sheet

For the dressing
250ml (9fl oz) tahini
125ml (4fl oz) rice vinegar
60ml (4 tbsp) olive oil
2 tbsp toasted sesame oil
2 tbsp grated fresh root ginger
4 tbsp lemon juice
2 tbsp tamari
½ tbsp wasabi powder or chilli flakes
   (optional)
3 tbsp coconut nectar

This salad is inspired by Asian flavours and packed full of nutrient-dense ingredients. The peppery watercress provides a burst of vitamins and is one of the power-greens that helps to boost immunity and provide high levels of calcium. The mixed seaweed contains minerals and has more nutritional value than any land vegetable. A delicious, zingy salad to pep up your taste buds. Eat this and be strong!

Mix together the cucumber marinade ingredients, pour it over the cucumber slices and leave to marinate for at least 30 minutes.

Rub ½ teaspoon of salt into the carrot sticks and set aside.

Put the mixed seaweed into a large bowl and cover with cold water. Allow to soak for 5–10 minutes, until softened. Drain in a colander, pat dry and place in a serving bowl. Make sure it is completely dry and not holding excess moisture.

Make the dressing by combining all the ingredients in a high-speed blender to form a thick, creamy-like consistency that will be the base of the dish. Spoon a tablespoon or so of the dressing on to the serving platter.

Mix the seaweed, carrot, daikon radish and watercress together. Squeeze lime juice over them. Taste and add salt if necessary.

Place the seaweed-watercress mixture in a mound in the centre of a bowl. Thin the dressing with a little water and drizzle it over the greens. Top with the marinated cucumber and drizzle with the remaining dressing.

Finish the dish by sprinkling over the toasted black sesame seeds, then cut the nori sheet into ribbons and place on top.

Farmacy Caesar Salad

Caesar salad is one of the greatest dishes when made well. It's hard to find a version that is truly plant-based, but we think this recipe nails the challenge well. This dish has been given the Farmacy makeover, combining olives, capers and lemons with our deep-tasting Alchemist's Sauce, creating a uniquely zesty Caesar dressing. It's completely oil-free, too. This dish works well as a starter or a main. It's a light, healthy salad which delivers on nutrition, with the Seaweed Broth and fresh green leaves providing a good-looking lunch or supper dish.

Serves 4
Preparation time: 15 minutes

For the Caesar dressing
3 tbsp lemon juice
1 garlic clove, crushed
7 Kalamata olives, pitted
1 tbsp capers
1 tsp lemon zest
1 tbsp Alchemist's Sauce (*see* page 70)
1 tbsp Philosopher's Sauce (*see* page 64)
1 tsp Dijon mustard
3 tbsp almond butter
2½ tbsp nutritional yeast
3 tbsp water

To serve
leaves of 1 baby Romaine lettuce
Alchemist's Sauce (*see* page 70)
lemon juice
chopped parsley
pepper

To make the dressing, add the crushed garlic to the lemon juice and allow to infuse for 10 minutes. Strain and discard the garlic.

Place all the dressing ingredients in a food processor except the almond butter, water and yeast. Process until smooth; about 10 seconds. Mix in the almond butter and water until you have a mayonnaise-like consistency; this takes about 4 minutes. Pour into a bowl and finish by mixing in the nutritional yeast by hand.

To serve, mix the lettuce leaves with a little Alchemist's Sauce and lemon juice and toss lightly. Add the dressing slowly until you have a good balance of leaves and dressing.

Finish the salad with chopped parsley and freshly ground pepper.

White Bean Salad

This had to be included in the salads that made the cut as it's one of our favourite dishes of all time. It's a light-tasting dish that's filling, too. It's quick to make once the beans are cooked. Even our friends who say they don't like white beans changed their minds after eating this. Everyone seems to love it – bean lovers and non-bean lovers. During the tasting sessions, more than one taster said afterwards, 'That was one of my favourite dishes and I thought I didn't like white beans!' It's a protein-rich recipe that gives an added boost of vitamin A. The apple cider vinegar helps digestion.

Serves 4

Preparation time: 5 minutes, plus bean preparation

1 carrot, diced

2 celery sticks, chopped

15g (½oz) rocket, coarsely chopped

500g (1lb 2oz) cooked white butter beans

green part of a spring onion, thinly sliced

1 tbsp Farmacy Seed Mix (*see* page 80)

2 tbsp sherry vinegar

1 tbsp apple cider vinegar

3 tbsp olive oil

2 large ripe tomatoes, quartered, seeds removed, flesh cubed

salt

Green Sauce (*see* page 66)

Place the carrot, celery, rocket and butter beans in a mixing bowl. Season with spring onion, the seed mix, 1 tablespoon of the sherry vinegar, the apple cider vinegar and the olive oil. Mix and allow to rest for at least 1 hour.

Season the tomato with salt and the remaining sherry vinegar.

To serve, pile the butter bean mixture into a single mound. Make a ring around the mound with the tomato cubes. Garnish with small drops of Green Sauce.

The Farmacy earth bowls are a centrepiece of our
food story, a one-world concept in which we use the
best flavours we can gather from all corners of this
beautiful planet. These are all dishes in which a
blend of flavours is served in one big bowl.

Earth Bowls

What is an Earth Bowl?

The ingredients in each of our earth bowls are carefully selected and combined to be health-supporting and delicious. Each recipe includes a gluten-free grain and three or four dishes combined to create a spectacular harmony of taste, colour and nutritional benefit. All the bowls come with a sauce to bind all of the ingredients together and are topped with fresh sprouts and/or seeds, which add goodness and colour to the dish. The recipes that follow in this section show how to make distinctive Earth Bowls and you can have fun creating a look that you love using a vibrant palette of different colours, tastes and textures.

Healthy fats

Avocado
Dried coconut
Nuts - almonds, cashews, walnuts, pecans
Seeds - sunflower, pumpkin, hemp, sesame

Raw items

Asparagus
Beetroot
Carrot
Cucumber
Fennel
Herbs
Radishes
Rocket
Salad leaves
Seaweed
Sprouts
Tomatoes
Watercress

Base

Grain - rice, millet
Kale
Leafy greens
Noodle - rice noodle, soba noodle
Seed - buckwheat, quinoa

Carbohydrate

Celeriac
Lotus root
Potatoes
Sweet potato

Cooked vegetables

Aubergine
Broccoli
Brussels sprouts
Cauliflower
Courgette
Kale
Peppers
Spinach

Legume

Black beans
Falafels
Garbanzo
Lentils
Mung beans

Farmacy Macro Bowl

Serves 4

**Preparation time: 30 minutes, plus
20 minutes cooking**

For the salad

olive oil, for roasting and dressing

1kg (2lb 4oz) sweet potatoes, cut into
2cm- (¾in-) cubes

1 head of broccoli, cut into bite-sized pieces

2 avocados, chopped into chunks

juice of 1 lime

15g (½oz) dried seaweed mix, soaked in
warm water

100g (3½oz) mixed greens (lamb's lettuce,
rocket and watercress)

100g (3½oz) mixed sprouts (radish, broccoli
and fenugreek)

juice of ½ lemon

225g (8oz) cooked quinoa (*see* page 51)

salt and black pepper

For the dressing

1 large courgette, peeled, chopped and
seeded

1 tbsp lemon juice

75ml (5 tbsp) Cashew Yogurt (*see* page 76)

1 tbsp Alchemist's Sauce (*see* page 70)

4 tbsp nutritional yeast

2 tsp chia seeds

3 pitted dates, soaked for 30 minutes

3 tbsp tamari

4 tbsp Vegetable Broth (*see* page 60)

1 chilli

3 tbsp chopped tarragon leaves

**This Farmacy classic is a nourishing bowl
with a focus on sea and land vegetables,
including sweet potato, seaweed and broccoli,
that has quinoa at its heart. This satisfying
meal will have you feeling wonderfully well-
fed and make sure that you leave the table
feeling energized. An everyday dish that gives
you all you want in a bowl and provides a
broad range of nutrients that the body needs,
including protein, vitamins, minerals and iron.**

Preheat the oven to 200°C (400°F), Gas Mark 6.

To prepare the salad, pour some olive oil into a baking tray, add
the sweet potato cubes and roast for 20 minutes until cooked
through, or longer if necessary. Sprinkle with salt and set aside.

Steam or boil the broccoli until al dente; about 6 minutes. Drain
and dress with a little oil and salt.

Dress the avocado chunks with lime juice and salt and set aside.

Drain the seaweed and pat dry thoroughly. Dress with a little olive
oil and salt.

Combine the greens and sprouts and dress with lemon juice.

Make the dressing by placing all the ingredients in a food processor
and blending until smooth.

To assemble, pile a small mound of the quinoa in the centre of the
bowl and arrange the sweet potato, greens and sprouts, avocado,
seaweed and broccoli around it. Stir the dressing well and serve
alongside the salad.

Kimchi Bowl

Serves 4

**Preparation time: 30 minutes, plus
20 minutes cooking**

6 spears white asparagus, peeled and cut
    into matchsticks

2 carrots, cut into matchsticks

200g (7oz) soba noodles

375g (13oz) Kimchi (*see* page 204)

30g (1oz) sprout mix

lemon juice, to season

For the mushrooms

500g (1lb 2oz) shiitake mushrooms

4 tbsp sesame oil, plus extra for the noodles

4 tbsp rice vinegar

1 garlic clove, left whole

2 tsp coconut nectar

handful of basil leaves

salt and black pepper, to taste

For the spinach stems

stems of 250g (9oz) spinach (choose stems
    attached to the root)

2 tbsp coconut oil

1 garlic clove, minced

1 chilli, minced

50g (1¾oz) dill (stems and leaves), chopped

zest and juice of 1 lime

For the dressing

3 garlic cloves, grated

6 tsp grated fresh root ginger

2 tbsp coconut nectar

2 chillies

2 tbsp brown rice miso

3 tbsp sesame oil

3 tbsp rice vinegar

2 tbsp lime juice

zest of 1 orange

1 tbsp Alchemist's Sauce (*see* page 70)

½ tsp chilli flakes

**This is a colourful kimchi and mushroom
bowl with a soba noodle base. The spinach
stems and dill are inspired by Turkish cooking
and mixed with Korean-inspired fermented
cabbage. The combination of flavours is
delightful. This bowl has a broad range of
vitamins and minerals and leaves you feeling
good after eating it. The kimchi helps to
support gut health and good digestion. This
bowl is served cold and makes a stunning
summer lunch or supper dish.**

Season the asparagus matchsticks with a little lemon juice and
soak the carrot matchsticks in water to make them softer.

To prepare the mushrooms sauté the mushrooms in the sesame
oil in a frying pan over a high heat until cooked but firm. In a
large bowl, combine the mushrooms, vinegar, garlic, coconut
nectar and basil and season with salt and pepper to taste.

Next sauté the spinach in the coconut oil in a frying pan over
a high heat until soft; about 10 minutes. Add the garlic, chilli,
chopped dill, lemon zest and juice. Season with salt and set aside.

Make the dressing by placing all the ingredients in a food processor
and blending until smooth. Season with salt and set aside.

Season the sprout mix with lemon juice and set aside.

Cook the noodles according to the packet instructions. Rinse
them in cold water to prevent them sticking together and run
your fingers through them to remove excess starch. Drizzle some
sesame oil over the noodles, toss and set aside.

To assemble, create a small mound of soba noodles on one side
of the serving dish. Arrange the asparagus, drained carrots, kimchi,
mushrooms, sprouts and spinach around it. Spoon the dressing
over the noodles and enjoy!

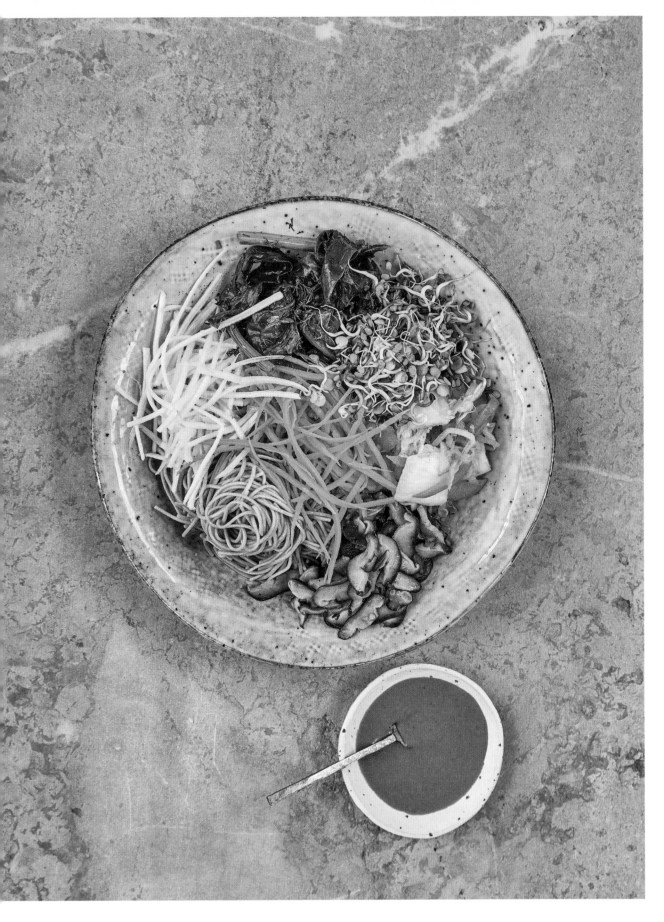

Kitchari Bowl

Serves 4
Preparation time: 30 minutes

375g (13oz) white basmati rice, cooked
sprouts, to garnish
1 quantity Cucumber Raita (*see* page 180)

For the mung beans
1 onion, diced
1 mild green chilli, cut into strips
2 tbsp olive oil
2 celery sticks, cut into 2cm (¾in) pieces
2 garlic cloves, chopped
1 small green chilli, thinly sliced (optional)
1cm (½in) piece of fresh root ginger, grated
1½ tbsp ground turmeric
2 tbsp Farmacy Seed Mix (*see* page 80)
2 tomatoes, cut into chunks
140g (5oz) split yellow mung beans, cooked

For the cauliflower
1 tsp mild curry powder
500g cauliflower, cut into 2.5cm (1in) florets
1 tbsp lemon juice
4 tbsp extra-virgin olive oil
salt and black pepper

For the mango chutney
1 ripe mango, cubed, liquid reserved
1 tbsp water
1 tbsp apple cider vinegar
1 tsp coconut nectar
1 red chilli, minced

For the greens
200g (7oz) rocket
1 avocado, sliced
2 tbsp shelled pistachios, toasted and
    chopped
2 tbsp olive oil
2 tbsp apple cider vinegar
salt and black pepper

This is an ancient recipe which has been given a Farmacy update, creating a classic, comforting dish that delivers a healthy and tasty hit in one bowl. Kitchari is an easily digestible bowl of nourishing ingredients that's gentle on the stomach. We have added a tomato jam and a spiced cauliflower side, enhancing the nutritional value as well as the flavour. The recipe uses split yellow mung beans, which don't have a gassy bean effect. There's protein, fibre and a healthy hit of vitamins in this vibrant bowl. White rice is recommended for quicker absorption, and is especially good for detoxing; any good-quality rice will work well in this dish.

To prepare the mung beans, sauté the onion and pepper in olive oil in a frying pan over a medium heat until translucent. Add the celery, garlic, chilli (if using), ginger, turmeric and seed mix and cook for 1 minute. Add the tomatoes and simmer until the mixture has a jam-like consistency. Remove from the heat, stir in the cooked mung beans and set aside.

To prepare the cauliflower, preheat the oven to 200°C (400°F), Gas Mark 6. Dry toast the curry powder for 1 minute in a hot frying pan without oil and set aside.

Put the cauliflower in a roasting tin and season with salt, pepper, the toasted curry powder and lemon juice. Add 3 tablespoons of olive oil. Roast in the oven for about 15 minutes, stirring once or twice. Set aside and allow to cool.

To make the chutney, sauté the mango briefly in a frying pan in its own liquid and the water until reduced. Add the vinegar, coconut nectar and chilli and cook for 1 minute more. The mix should not be runny. Set aside.

To prepare the greens, mix all the ingredients together.

Assemble the bowl by piling a mound of rice in the centre and arranging all the side dishes around it. Garnish with sprouts.

Japanese Bowl

Serves 4
Preparation time: 25 minutes

For the lotus root

1 lotus root (*see* Notes below) cut into
    0.5cm- (¼in-) thick slices
2 tbsp olive oil
salt

For the almond miso sauce

1 tbsp brown rice miso
3 tbsp almond butter
4 tbsp fresh apple juice
1 tsp maple syrup
1cm (½in) slice of fresh root ginger, grated
4 tbsp water

For the spinach

200g (7oz) spinach
4 tbsp Seaweed Broth (*see* page 61)
1 tbsp tamari
½ tsp coconut nectar
1 tbsp lime juice

For the beans, seaweed and asparagus

200g (7oz) green beans
12 thin asparagus spears
100g (3½oz) mixed seaweed (wakame, dulse
    or any other ready-to-use seaweed), soaked
1 tbsp rice vinegar
2 tbsp lemon juice
2 tbsp sesame oil, plus extra for the noodles
2 tbsp sesame seeds

250g (9oz) black rice noodles
4 radishes, thinly sliced

A bowl inspired by oriental flavours that delivers a powerhouse of nutritional hits from the sprouts, asparagus and seaweed broth. The apple, ginger and almond in the sauce give this dish a unique edge and flavour. Raw live sprouts contain good levels of fibre, potassium, copper and iron. Other important minerals come from the impressive lotus root. This dish is best served cold.

Preheat the oven to 180°C (350°F), Gas Mark 4.

Put the lotus root on a baking tray with the oil, season with salt and bake in the oven for 20 minutes.

Prepare the sauce by mixing all the ingredients together in a bowl. Set aside. If you like, you can adjust the consistency of the sauce later by adding a little more water.

Put the spinach in a small saucepan, add a little boiling water and cook briefly. Mix the other ingredients to create a dressing. Lightly dress the spinach (you may not need all of the dressing). Set aside.

Boil the beans and the asparagus in separate saucepans until al dente and put them on one side. Drain the seaweed.

Mix the rice vinegar with 1 tablespoon of lemon juice and the sesame oil and add to the beans along with the seaweed. Sprinkle with sesame seeds and set aside. Season the sprouts with the remaining lemon juice.

Cook the noodles according to the packet instructions. Refresh them in cold water and run them through your fingers to remove excess starch. Allow to cool and then dry and dress lightly with 1 tablespoon of sesame oil.

To assemble, place a small mound of noodles in the bowl. Arrange the beans, spinach, asparagus and radishes around them. Top with lotus root and some sprouts and serve with the sauce.

Notes

The delicately flavoured root of the lotus plant has been popular for centuries in Japan and China. Break the root at the intersections of the individual parts, then wash thoroughly in cold water. Trim the ends and peel off the rough outer skin. Rinse in lemon water (or vinegar) to prevent discoloration.

Mexican Bowl

Serves 4
Preparation time: 20 minutes

250g (9oz) cooked brown rice

50g (1¾oz) chopped coriander (stems and leaves)

70g (2½oz) dry toasted pumpkin seeds

For the beans

1 tbsp olive oil

½ onion, diced

125g (4½oz) red pepper, diced

25g (1oz) celery, diced

1 garlic clove, minced

1 small tomato, seeded and diced

350g (12oz) cooked black beans

500ml (18fl oz) Vegetable Broth (*see* page 60)

salt and black pepper

For the avocado and tomato salsa

1 ripe avocado, cubed

2 medium tomatoes, cubed

1 tbsp apple cider vinegar

1 garlic clove, grated

2 tbsp chopped coriander leaves

2 tbsp lime juice

salt, to season

For the courgette

1 large courgette, cubed

1 tsp smoked paprika

salt, to season

To garnish

100g (3½oz) mixed greens

lemon juice, to taste

olive oil

6 tbsp Cashew Yogurt (*see* page 76)

50g (1¾oz) sprouts

2 tbsp Farmacy Seed Mix (*see* page 80)

A best-seller in our restaurant, this is a filling, one-bowl wonder that delivers on taste. We've adapted the recipe to make it easy to prepare at home, while keeping the Mexican-inspired flavours. The beans contain high levels of protein and minerals, there are good fats in the avocado and healthy-gut probiotics in the yogurt. The flavours are deep and satisfying and this remains one of our favourites to savour and enjoy slowly for lunch or supper; a dish to share with some lucky friends.

Make sure the cooked rice is completely cold, then mix with the coriander and pumpkin seeds. Set aside.

Prepare the beans by sautéing the onion, red pepper, celery and garlic in the olive oil in a heavy-based saucepan over a medium-high heat until the onions are translucent. Add the tomatoes and cook for 1 minute. Add the beans and the broth and bring to the boil. Reduce to a simmer and cook slowly until greatly reduced, taking care not to let it burn. Season with salt and pepper and set aside.

For the avocado and the tomato salsa, mix all the ingredients and set aside.

To prepare the courgette, preheat the oven to 180°C (350°F), Gas Mark 4. Place the courgette cubes on a baking tray, season with paprika and salt and roast for 10 minutes until al dente.

Dress the mixed greens with a splash of lemon juice and a little olive oil and set aside.

Make a mound of rice in the centre of a serving dish and place the other dishes around it. Spoon on the cashew yogurt, sprinkle with sprouts and the seed mix and serve.

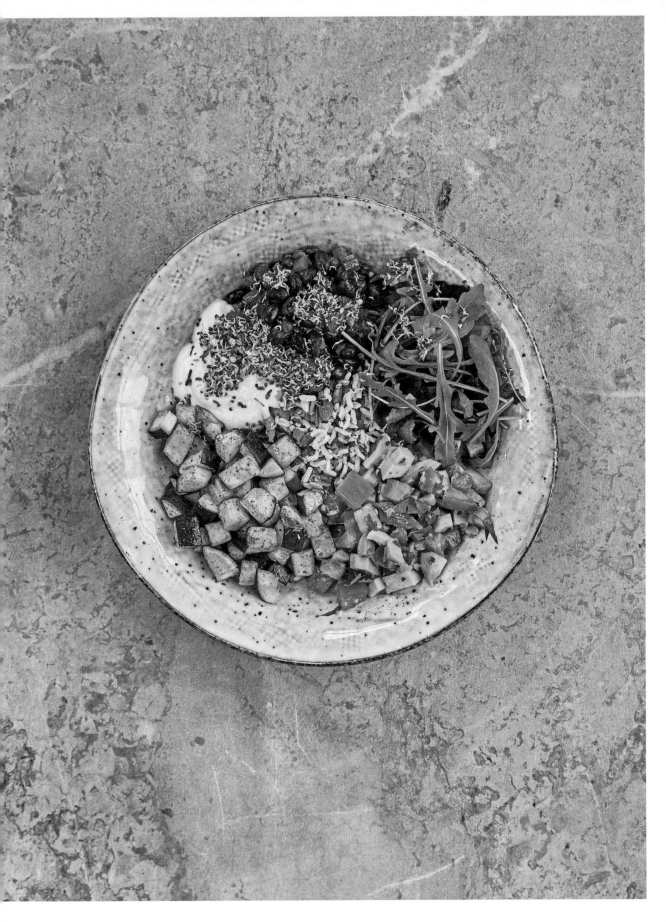

Thai Bowl

Serves 4
**Preparation time: 30 minutes, plus
24 hours pickling**

For the pickled cabbage
500g (1lb 2oz) red cabbage, thinly sliced
125ml (4fl oz) apple cider vinegar
65ml (4½ tbsp) rice vinegar
2 tsp coconut nectar
2 garlic cloves, crushed
2 tsp pickling seeds (mustard, fennel,
    coriander or caraway, or a mixture)
1½ tbsp salt, plus extra for the noodles
black pepper

For the sauce
4 tbsp lime juice, plus 2 limes to serve
2 tbsp Philosopher's Sauce (*see* page 64)
2 tbsp tamarind paste
3 tsp coconut nectar
1 tbsp tamari
1 chilli, crushed (optional)
2 garlic cloves, finely chopped
1cm (½in) piece of fresh root ginger, grated
7 tbsp water
1 tbsp sesame oil, plus extra for the noodles
2 tbsp almond butter
3 basil leaves, torn

For the vegetables
2 carrots, cut into matchsticks
1 courgette, cut into matchsticks
100g (3½oz) sprouts
4 pak choi, shredded
1 ripe avocado, cubed

325g (11½oz) rice noodles

To garnish
coriander leaves
toasted peanuts

This bowl is inspired by Thailand's great national dish, pad Thai, and the flavours of the vibrant street food of Bangkok. The ingredients have anti-inflammatory properties and the chilli and spices aid digestion and support gut health. Enjoy the flavours of Asia in this heart-warming bowl.

Prepare the pickled cabbage a day ahead by sprinkling 1 tablespoon of salt over the cabbage and massaging the salt thoroughly into it. Let it rest for half an hour.

Make the pickling liquid by mixing the rest of the ingredients in a large, screw-top jar. Shake vigorously until well mixed. Pour over the cabbage and allow to marinate for 24 hours.

Transfer the mixture to a clean jar (it should be large enough to hold all of the ingredients with a 4cm/1½in gap at the top) and refrigerate.

The following day prepare the sauce by mixing together all the ingredients. Set aside.

Prepare the vegetables. Mix together the carrots, courgette and sprouts and set aside.

Put the pak choi in a large heatproof bowl and pour a kettleful of boiling water over it. Let it stand for a moment, then strain and set aside to cool before combining with the avocado.

Cook the noodles according to the packet instructions. Refresh in cold water and run your fingers through them to wash away the excess starch. Rinse a couple of times in this way, then strain and spread them over a cutting board. As soon as they are dry, dress with 1 tablespoon of sesame oil and a sprinkle of salt.

Place a small mound of noodles in the centre of the bowl. Add the pickled cabbage, vegetable mix, pak choi and avocado. Top with roasted peanuts and coriander leaves. Serve with half a lime to squeeze over and the sauce on the side.

Middle Eastern Bowl

Serves 4

**Preparation time: 40 minutes, plus
15 minutes cooking and refrigeration**

For the millet tabbouleh

2 garlic cloves, finely chopped

zest of ½ lemon

200g (7oz) mint leaves, finely chopped

100g (3½oz) parsley or rocket, or both

60g (2¼oz) toasted hazelnuts, chopped

350g (12oz) cooked millet

1½ tsp salt

black pepper

For the cucumber salad

2 cucumbers, chopped

2 garlic cloves, finely chopped

3 tbsp fresh lemon juice

3 tbsp olive oil

3 tbsp chopped coriander

For the aubergine

150g (5½oz) aubergine, sliced

For the tomato salad

2 medium tomatoes, chopped

1cm (½in) slice of lemon, seeded and
finely chopped

1 tsp Farmacy Seed Mix (*see* page 80)

1 tbsp apple cider vinegar

2 tbsp chopped coriander (stems and leaves)

For the fattoush dressing

4 tbsp olive oil

4 tbsp tomato juice

½ tsp finely chopped garlic

3 tbsp lemon juice

1 chilli, finely chopped (optional)

To serve

Farmacy Hummus (*see* page 111)

mixed greens

sprouts

This nourishing bowl features the Farmacy version of tabbouleh using millet instead of wheat. The tabbouleh is so delicious that we want to make it constantly just to eat on its own. It tastes even better if refrigerated and eaten the next day (use a little more seasoning if you do this). The fattoush dressing adds a Middle Eastern zing.

Start the tabbouleh. In a bowl, stir together the garlic, lemon zest, mint, parsley or rocket, hazelnuts, salt and pepper. Set aside.

For the cucumber salad, place the chopped cucumbers on kitchen paper to dry. Mix the rest of the ingredients to create a dressing. Dress the cucumber pieces and set aside.

Cook the aubergines as described in the Aubergine Steaks recipe (*see* page 186), but skip the salting step. Set aside.

Prepare the tomato salad by mixing all the ingredients. Set aside.

Put all the ingredients for the fattoush dressing into a screw-topped jar and shake vigorously.

Before serving, finish the tabbouleh. Make sure the millet is completely cold so that it will not wilt the herbs. Combine it with the lemon, herb and hazelnut mixture using a fork.

Take a serving plate and place a small mound of millet off-centre towards the edge of the plate. Place some aubergine, hummus, tomato salad, greens and cucumber salad around it in a half moon shape. Top with sprouts and serve with the dressing on the side.

Here's a selection of our favourite main courses, including an adaptation of the famous Farmacy burger. These are dishes to delight and share, ranging from easy suppers to more elaborate dinner party recipes to eat with friends.

Mains

Sweet Potato & Mushroom Curry

Serves 4
**Preparation time: 15 minutes, plus
20 minutes cooking**

For the curry paste

1 red chilli

4 garlic cloves, coarsely chopped

2 lemon grass stalks, sliced

4 coriander sprigs, stems included

1½ tsp ground turmeric

1 tsp salt

For the curry

4 shallots, chopped

4 garlic cloves, chopped

2 tbsp olive oil

2 tbsp curry paste (*see* above)

1 tbsp grated fresh root ginger

500ml (18fl oz) Vegetable Broth (*see* page 60)

1kg (2lb 4oz) sweet potatoes, peeled and
cubed

2 kaffir lime leaves, chopped

200g (7oz) oyster or other mushrooms

125g (4½oz) roasted peanuts, chopped

375ml (13fl oz) coconut milk

3 tbsp Philosopher's Sauce (*see* page 64)

2 tbsp coconut nectar

For the cucumber raita

2 cucumbers, seeded and diced

125ml (4fl oz) Cashew Yogurt (*see* page 76)

3 tbsp chopped dill

1½ tbsp lemon juice

To garnish

dry toasted pumpkin seeds

coriander leaves

2 limes, halved

**This Thai-inspired recipe is a homely update
on our Farmacy restaurant curry. It's colourful
and bursting with goodness. Susie says that
this curry would be her desert island luxury.
This is one of the recipes that elicited excited
gasps at the testing table. Its flavour is deep
and delicious, warming heart and soul.**

Blend together all the curry paste ingredients in a food processor
until they form a paste. You may need to add a couple tablespoons
of water. Set aside. This will make more paste than you need for
this recipe, but it will last several months if refrigerated.

To make the curry, sauté the shallots and garlic in the oil in
a heavy-based saucepan over a medium heat until they are
translucent. Do not let them colour. Add the curry paste and
ginger and cook for 1 minute.

Add the vegetable broth, sweet potatoes and lime leaves and
bring to the boil. Reduce the heat and cook for 10 minutes.

Then add the mushrooms, the peanuts and the coconut milk.
Stir in the philosopher's sauce and the coconut nectar. Allow to
simmer for 5 minutes. Test whether the sweet potatoes are done
and simmer longer if necessary.

Turn off the heat under the saucepan, cover and allow to rest for
20 minutes.

Meanwhile, make the raita by combining all of the ingredients in
a medium-sized bowl.

Serve the curry garnished with pumpkin seeds and coriander leaves
along with a dollop of raita, and half a lime for squeezing over.

Farmacy Burger

The number one choice on our restaurant menu, so we just couldn't leave it out. This is our plant-based take on the ubiquitous burger. It's full of flavour and nourishing too. We use black beans to create the delicious taste of the bean burger, supplying protein, magnesium and vitamins. The other layers are tasty additions that, piled together, create this iconic dish with a heart. It's a winner!

Serves 8

Preparation time: 40 minutes, plus 30 minutes refrigeration and 10 minutes cooking

For the burger

280g (10oz) portobello mushrooms
60g (2¼oz) red pepper, chopped
30g (1oz) red onion, chopped
30g (1oz) brown rice miso
60g (2¼oz) gluten-free jumbo oat flakes
¼ tsp ground black pepper
pinch of salt
¼ tsp garlic powder
¼ tsp chilli powder
15g (½oz) brown rice flour
1½ tbsp olive oil
375g (13oz) cooked black beans (*see* page 57)
125g (4½oz) cooked millet (*see* page 51)
10g (¼oz) parsley, chopped

To assemble

8 sourdough burger buns
Goji Ketchup (*see* page 112)
1 small round lettuce
Alioli (*see* page 114)
1 large ripe tomato, sliced
1 jar organic pickles
1 avocado, mashed

Preheat the oven to 180°C (350°F), Gas Mark 4.

Put the mushrooms on a baking tray and cook in the oven for 10 minutes. Take them out, drain the juice into a jug and set both to one side to cool.

Put the pepper and onion on another baking tray and cook for 15 minutes. Set aside to cool.

Place the cooled vegetables in a food processor and blend. Add the remaining burger ingredients except the millet and parsley and blend again, being careful not to overprocess the mixture or it can turn into a paste.

Finally, add the millet and parsley and stir through.

Cool the mixture in the refrigerator, then take out and shape into 8 individual burgers.

Heat a griddle or frying pan over a high heat until hot. Cook the burgers until a little crust forms underneath, about 5 minutes, turning once.

Cut the buns in half and toast them if you like. Spoon a tablespoon of goji ketchup on to the base of each bun and add a layer of lettuce leaves, followed by a burger. Add a layer of alioli then a slice of tomato and a couple of slices of pickle. Finally, spread mashed avocado on the underside of each bun top and place on top.

Broccoli & Cabbage with Coconut Sauce

GF NF VG

This is a beautiful dish of nutrient-loaded vegetables with a gorgeous colour which is inspired by a vegetable dish served by Damien Bolger in his Barcelona restaurant. Here we take two ordinary vegetables and combine them in a coconut-based sauce to create a taste sensation. The addition of dill and lime give this dish a herby zing.

Serves 4
**Preparation time: 30 minutes plus
  20 minutes cooking**

For the dill oil
100g (3½oz) dill
200ml (7fl oz) sunflower or grapeseed oil
1 tsp salt

For the cabbage and broccoli
1 head broccoli, cut into florets
4 tbsp coconut oil
16 Chinese (napa) cabbage leaves
500ml (18fl oz) coconut milk
1 tbsp Philosopher's Sauce (*see* page 64)
squeeze of lime juice
salt and black pepper

To serve
175g (6oz) cooked quinoa (*see* page 51)
dill sprigs
zest of 1 lime

For the dill oil, bring a saucepan of water to the boil and briefly blanch the dill, then remove with a slotted spoon and refresh in a bowl of iced water. (Keep both the boiling and iced water to cook and cool the cabbage.) Place the dill in a blender with the oil and salt and blend on high for 2–3 minutes. Strain off the oil and reserve for later.

In a frying pan, sauté the broccoli florets in the coconut oil, allowing them to char a little. While the florets are still al dente, turn off heat under the pan and allow them to finish cooking while the pan cools. Set aside.

Blanch the cabbage leaves in boiling, salted water, then refresh in iced water and drain in a colander.

Pour the coconut milk into a saucepan, bring to the boil and reduce by half. Add the Philosopher's Sauce and stir. Add the cabbage leaves, the broccoli, a little dill oil and the lime juice and season with salt and pepper.

Serve with the quinoa, garnished with dill sprigs, lime zest and some dill oil.

Aubergine Steaks with Tahini & Green Sauce

GF NF VG

These vegetable steaks have a potent flavour and are enhanced by two of our favourite Farmacy sauces – Tahini and Green Sauce. This is a light dish loaded with flavour. Aubergine is a nutrient-packed vegetable that works well served as vegetable steaks. It can be ruined by cooking it in too much oil. In this recipe, the aubergine is cooked by steaming after being briefly browned in a little oil. It is delicious served with a light salad.

Serves 4
**Preparation time: 10 minutes, plus
  30 minutes draining**

3 firm aubergines, cut into 2cm (¾in) slices
4 tbsp olive oil
4 tbsp water
salt

To serve
Tahini Sauce (*see* page 68)
Green Sauce (*see* page 66)

Salt the aubergine slices generously to draw out the moisture. This will release any bitterness and shorten the cooking time.

Place the slices vertically in a colander and leave them to stand in the sink for 30 minutes or longer.

When you're ready to cook, take some kitchen paper and wipe the salt and any moisture from the surface of the slices.

Cook the aubergine slices in 2 batches. Brush half of the slices with 1 tablespoon of olive oil, and heat another tablespoon of oil in a nonstick frying pan over a high heat. Put the oiled slices in the hot frying pan, turning them after 3 minutes. Add 2 tablespoons of water to the pan, cover and reduce the heat to medium low for 4 minutes. Repeat with the remaining slices.

Spoon some Tahini Sauce on to a serving plate, place 3 or 4 overlapping aubergine slices over the sauce and dollop some Green Sauce on top. This dish can be served either warm or cold.

Forager's Pie

A Farmacy stew with a simple, fresh-tasting topping. This dish supplies good levels of fibre and vitamins. Fennel is a great source of calcium, magnesium and iron and the puréed celeriac topping creates a lighter version of a traditional family pie. Best made with really fresh ingredients.

Serves 4

Preparation time: 20 minutes plus 40 minutes cooking

For the stew

200g (7oz) white onion, soaked in cold water for 30 minutes then thinly sliced

5 tbsp olive oil

5 small globe artichokes, peeled, chokes removed and quartered (*see* Notes below)

1½ tbsp lemon juice (to be used in preparation of the artichoke hearts)

200g (7oz) young fennel bulb, cut into small cubes

50g (1¾oz) fresh dill

500g (1lb 2oz) asparagus spears, cut into 1cm (½in) pieces

500g (1lb 2oz) oyster mushrooms, sliced

½ tsp salt

For the celeriac

1kg (2lb 4oz) celeriac, peeled and cut into large cubes

2 tbsp olive oil

salt

To garnish (optional)

microgreens or sprouts

fennel fronds

Heat a large, ovenproof dish over a medium-low heat and cook the onion in a little of the oil until it becomes translucent. Reduce the heat under the pan to cook the onion without colouring it.

Add the artichokes, fennel and dill and stir well. Cover and cook for 5 minutes, then add 3 tablespoons of water and stir. Cover and cook for another 10 minutes.

At this point the artichokes should be more than half cooked. Add the asparagus spears, mushrooms and salt and stir. Check the liquid in the pan; there should be a little moisture to continue cooking the vegetables, but if it's dry, add 1 or 2 more tablespoons of water and cover.

Check again after 10 minutes. There should be a little vegetable syrup in the bottom of the pan. If there is too much liquid, strain it off into another saucepan and reduce it before returning it to the vegetables. Cover, remove from the heat and set aside.

Heat a large saucepan of water until boils, add the celeriac cubes and cook until tender. Transfer to a food processor with the olive oil and salt to taste. The celeriac should have the consistency of mashed potato.

Top the cooked vegetables with the celeriac and cook under a preheated hot grill until the pie is warmed through and the topping is golden and crispy.

To serve, spoon on to a plate and garnish with microgreens and fennel fronds, if liked.

Notes

To clean and prepare artichokes, cut them in half and peel back the outer leaves until you can see the tender interior. Clean the fuzz around the artichoke heart and trim away the tougher parts. Dab the remaining heart with lemon juice to prevent oxidation.

Mushrooms & Chard Stems with Tarragon Sauce

Serves 4

Preparation time: 20 minutes, plus 15 minutes cooking

For the millet

3 tbsp lemon juice

5 tbsp olive oil

½ tsp salt

100g (3½oz) parsley, finely chopped

175g (6oz) cooked millet, cooled (*see* page 51)

For the tarragon sauce

125ml (4fl oz) Cashew Yogurt (*see* page 76)

1 tbsp pine nuts

1½ tbsp lemon juice

3 tbsp tarragon leaves

2 tbsp olive oil

For the walnut and lime sauce

70g (2½oz) walnuts

3 tbsp walnut oil

70g (2½oz) mixed herbs (tarragon, parsley, chives, rocket)

4 tbsp lime juice

½ green chilli (optional)

For the mushrooms and asparagus

300g (10½oz) wild mushrooms

2 tbsp olive oil

1 garlic clove, finely chopped

8 white asparagus spears, cut into thick matchsticks and tips split

3 tbsp lemon juice

150g (5½oz) Swiss chard stems, cut into sticks (keep the leaves for Farm Green Soup – *see* page 132)

salt

This classic dish was inspired by a walk in the woods. It's a perfect spring or autumn supper dish. The recipe is created from a forager's basket of asparagus, mushrooms and chard stems flavoured with tarragon, millet and nuts. Millet has many nutrients, including calcium, iron, zinc and magnesium, as well as being a healthy source of essential fats, protein and fibre. This is a filling dish that looks beautiful. It works well as a dinner party main course and is even better eaten al fresco.

Mix together the lemon juice, oil and salt to create a dressing for the millet. Mix in the parsley and cold millet and set aside.

Prepare the tarragon sauce by mixing all the ingredients in a blender until smooth.

Prepare the walnut and lime sauce by blending all the ingredients in a food processor until smooth.

Heat a frying pan over a medium high heat and sauté the mushrooms in half the olive oil. Move them as little as possible to allow a crust to form. Once they are well coloured, stir once, add the garlic, swirl for 30 seconds and set aside. Sauté the asparagus spears in half the remaining oil until they are al dente. Season with salt and a squeeze of lemon juice and add to the mushrooms.

Next sauté the chard stems in the remaining oil until cooked. A little charring is fine. Season with salt and add to the mushrooms. Toss together until all the elements are combined.

To serve, spoon a scant tablespoon of walnut and lime sauce on to a serving plate and top with the millet and mushroom asparagus mixture and chard. Garnish with generous dollops of tarragon sauce.

Butternut Squash & Spinach Casserole

A hearty casserole with deep flavours, ideal for any season. This dish can be eaten hot in the winter or served deliciously cold in summer. The nuts, squash and spinach provide vitamins, fibre, zinc, protein, folate, potassium and other minerals. For this recipe choose a squash with a long neck which will give you even round slices.

Serves 4

Preparation time: 30 minutes, plus soaking and 45 minutes cooking

For the cashew cream

200g (7oz) raw cashews, soaked for 2 hours, then drained

4 tbsp lemon juice

½ tsp salt

1 tbsp nutritional yeast

150ml (5fl oz) water

For the squash

neck of 1 large butternut squash, peeled and sliced in 0.5cm (¼in) rounds

1 tbsp coconut oil

salt and black pepper

100g (3½oz) crushed macadamia nuts

For the white sauce

2 tbsp olive oil, plus extra for the dish

200g (7oz) spinach

1 garlic clove, minced

100ml (3½fl oz) Vegetable Broth (*see* page 60)

100ml coconut milk

1 tbsp almond butter

1 tsp salt

¼ tsp pepper

pinch of grated nutmeg

Place all the ingredients for the cashew cream in a food processor and blend until the mixture has a creamy texture. Add a little more water if needed to create a good consistency. Set aside.

Preheat the oven to 180°C (350°F), Gas Mark 4 and line 2 baking sheets with greaseproof paper.

Put the squash slices in a bowl and toss with some of the coconut oil. Arrange the squash pieces on the prepared baking sheets, brush with more coconut oil and season with salt and pepper. Bake in the oven for 15 minutes or until barely tender. Leave the oven on to bake the finished dish.

To make the white sauce, heat the olive oil in a sauté pan and cook the spinach. Remove from the pan and put it on a board to dry. Gently pat the leaves dry if necessary with kitchen paper; the spinach must be completely dry or it will water down the sauce. Use the same pan to cook the garlic for 1 minute. Add the broth, coconut milk and almond butter and stir to make a thick sauce. Mix in the spinach, season with salt, pepper and nutmeg. Set aside.

Lightly oil a medium-sized, shallow ovenproof dish. Arrange a layer of about 10 overlapping butternut squash pieces on the bottom of the dish, then pour over some cashew cream. Repeat until you have 2 or 3 layers. Cover with the white sauce and sprinkle the macadamia nuts on top.

Cover the casserole with greaseproof paper and bake in the oven until heated through; about 10 minutes. Uncover and cook for a further 4 minutes before serving.

The side dishes in this chapter give a blast of
taste and colour to complement any table. Healthy
and nutritious, with style and crunch, these are
perfect for sharing and combining with main courses.

Sides

Sweet Potato Home Fries

This recipe offers a healthy alternative to deep-fried chips. These chips provide all the nutritional benefits of the sweet potato, including potassium, dietary fibre and plenty of vitamin C. Sage and garlic add an Italian touch and the sprout garnish contributes another nutritional layer.

Serves 4

Preparation time: 10 minutes, plus 35 minutes cooking

1kg (2lb 4oz) sweet potatoes, cubed
2 tbsp olive oil, plus a little extra
6 sage leaves, torn into pieces
1 garlic clove, finely chopped
handful of lentil sprouts, to garnish
salt

For the dressing
2 tbsp olive oil
2 tbsp apple cider vinegar
¼ tsp salt

Put the sweet potatoes into a saucepan of salted boiling water for 3 minutes. Drain and allow to cool slightly.

Heat the olive oil in a frying pan until very hot, then add the sweet potato. Sear until a crust begins to form on the potatoes. Reduce the heat to minimum and allow the crust to develop without moving the cubes.

After 5 minutes, check that the heat is low enough not to burn the cubes, but hot enough to continue forming a crust. After 10 minutes, turn the cubes to cook their other sides. Repeat until all sides of the cubes have a crust. Don't move them too often as that prevents a crust forming.

After 20 minutes, add a little more oil to the frying pan along with the sage leaves and toss. After another 5 minutes, add the garlic and toss again. Remove from the heat.

Make the dressing by combining the ingredients in a screw-top jar and shaking it vigorously.

Toss the sprouts with the sweet potato cubes and serve with the dressing.

Baked Chickpea Sticks

GF NF VG

These chickpea sticks taste as good as they look and their crispness comes from being baked. Chickpeas are high in protein as well as fibre, and, like all the dishes in the Farmacy kitchen, they are gluten-free and taste divine. The sticks are made from chickpea flour, retaining all the nutrients, and they are a great source of plant-based iron. These are fun to eat and great to share – perfect as party food or a pre-dinner snack.

Serves 6

Preparation time: 20 minutes, plus 2 hours refrigeration

115g (4oz) chickpea flour
500ml (18fl oz) cold water
1 tsp salt
1 chilli
1 tsp Farmacy Seed Mix (*see* page 80)
½ tsp lemon zest
¼ tsp garlic powder
1 tbsp olive oil, plus extra for cooking

To garnish (all optional)
sesame seeds
paprika
chopped herbs
Tahini Sauce (*see* page 68)

Blend all the ingredients together in a food processor until smooth. Transfer the contents to a saucepan and cook over a low heat, stirring continuously, for about 10 minutes. You will end up with a consistency similar to clotted cream or thick porridge.

Pour into an oiled baking dish and refrigerate until set. This takes about 2 hours.

Preheat the oven to 180°C (350°F), Gas Mark 4. Remove the mixture from the dish and cut into chip shapes. Place on an oiled baking tray to prevent them sticking and bake until they are golden brown; about 30 minutes.

Serve sprinkled with sesame seeds, paprika and chopped fresh herbs, or dip in Tahini Sauce.

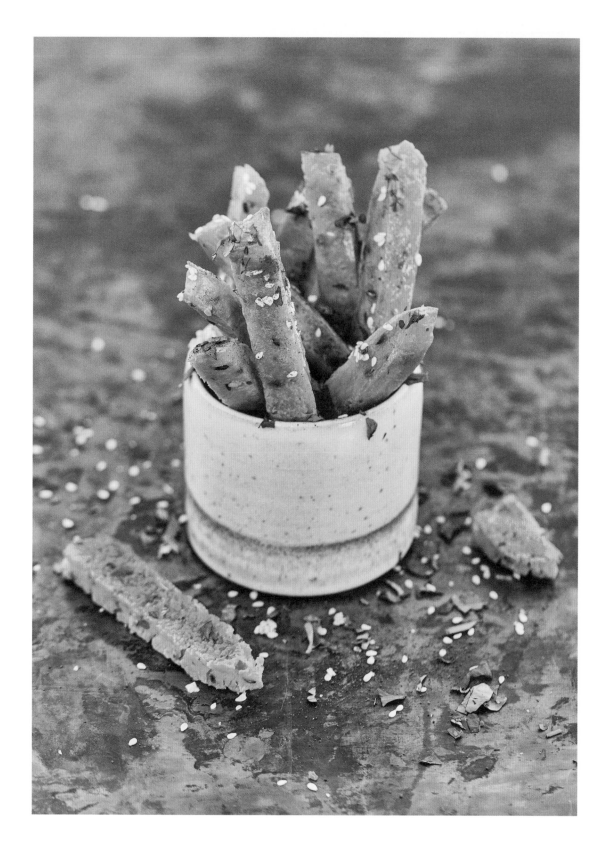

Roasted Red Pepper Confit

The smoky sweetness inside red peppers is brought out in this recipe, which is high in antioxidants. If your body is in need of some extra iron, try combining peppers with your regular iron source as they can significantly help iron absorption. Red peppers are also a great source of vitamin B6, they contain more than twice the recommended daily intake of vitamin C and are known to help increase metabolic rate. This vibrant red dish will add a splash of colour to any table. We use this confit in other Farmacy recipes, including the Green Salad with Lentil Dressing (*see* page 144).

Serves 4–6
Preparation time: 5 minutes, plus 40 minutes cooking

1 tbsp olive oil

3 red peppers, cut into strips

1–2 red chillies, finely chopped

1–2 garlic cloves

1 tsp tamari

1 tbsp sherry vinegar

3 tbsp water, plus extra if needed

1 tbsp coconut nectar

salt

Heat the olive oil in a lidded wok and add the pepper strips. Toss them gently until the strips are covered in oil. Sprinkle a little salt over them.

After 5 minutes, add the rest of the ingredients and gently toss again. Bring to the boil, reduce the heat, cover and allow to simmer. Stir occasionally and then increasingly often as the liquid in the wok disappears.

Make sure that the peppers don't stick to the wok. If they are not completely soft, add a little more water and continue to cook. The peppers are ready when they are sweet and tender and all the liquid has evaporated. The whole process takes 30–40 minutes.

Roasted Broccoli with Chilli & Garlic

A spicy side dish that delivers great taste and lots of nutrients. An easy way to spruce up broccoli and a good source of fibre, protein, iron, calcium and vitamin C.

Serves 4

Preparation time: 5 minutes, plus 15 minutes roasting

1 head of broccoli, cut into florets
1–2 red chillies, minced
1–2 garlic cloves, minced
olive oil
2 tbsp nutritional yeast
salt

Preheat the oven to 190°C (375°F), Gas Mark 5.

In a bowl combine all the ingredients except the nutritional yeast. Tip them on to a baking tray and roast them in the oven for about 15 minutes.

Sprinkle with the nutritional yeast and serve

Green Apple & Black Garlic Kimchi

Kimchi is good for the gut and the taste buds and can be made easily at home. It supports the general health of the body and benefits the gut as a result of the fermentation process. Fermented foods are rich in enzymes that support the immune system, help with digestion and keep the pH of the gut in an optimum balance. The green apple adds a delicious, sharper taste to the mixture when combined with the black garlic, which contributes further health benefits, and creates a great flavour without adding onions.

Serves 8

Preparation time: 1 hour, plus 3–5 days fermentation

1 Chinese (napa) cabbage, about 1kg (2lb 4oz), cut into 2cm (¾in) segments

85g (3oz) salt

3 red chillies, or whatever you have to hand

1 tsp grated fresh root ginger

2 black garlic cloves

1 tightly-packed tbsp finely chopped regular garlic

1½ tsp coconut nectar

3 tbsp water

1 green apple, cut into matchsticks

300g (10½oz) daikon, cut into matchsticks

Combine the cabbage with the salt, rubbing in the salt for 5 minutes. Allow to stand for 1 hour.

Put the cabbage in a colander and rinse 3 times to thoroughly rinse out the salt. Leave in the colander for 20 minutes.

In a blender, make a paste from the chillies, ginger, black garlic, regular garlic, coconut nectar and water.

Mix the cabbage, paste, apples and daikon in a large bowl. Transfer the mixture to a 1.5 litre (2½ pint) jar with a well-fitting lid.

Carefully press down the mixture to release any air bubbles and create a tightly packed column. Leave about 3cm (1¼in) space at the top of the jar and make sure the mixture is completely submerged in the liquid.

Seal the jar loosely (tightly sealed jars could explode when opened) and store in a cool, dry place in a bowl to catch any overflow. Leave to ferment for 3 to 5 days.

Check the fermentation every day and remove the lid to release air bubbles and any pressure in the jar. Remember to loosely seal the jar again afterwards.

Pak Choi in Yogurt Dressing

This is inspired by a classic Thai pak choi dish. We've added avocado and homemade yogurt to create a creamier, more nutritious and thicker sauce. Pak choi is a leafy vegetable that has played a large part in Asian cuisine and in traditional Chinese medicine. This dish is a great source of calcium, magnesium and iron, supplying antioxidants and nutrients to help with strong bones, as well as benefitting heart health and immunity. Pak choi cooks fast, making this light and versatile side quick to put together.

Serves 4
Preparation time: 5 minutes

4 heads of pak choi, shredded
1 ripe avocado, cubed

For the dressing
250ml (9fl oz) coconut or Cashew Yogurt (*see* page 76)
2 tbsp Philosopher's Sauce (*see* page 64)
2 tbsp lime juice, or to taste

To garnish
2 tbsp crushed roasted peanuts
2 tbsp black sesame seeds

Put the pak choi in a large heatproof bowl and pour a kettleful of boiling water over it. Let it stand for a moment, then strain and set aside.

Prepare the dressing by mixing together the yogurt, Philosopher's Sauce and lime juice. It should taste distinctly of lime, so adjust to taste.

Mix the avocado with the pak choi and the dressing. Top with the crushed peanuts and sesame seeds and serve on a beautiful plate.

Asian Slaw

This light, crunchy slaw can be served alongside a variety of dishes to add colour, flavour and a burst of healthy nutrients including protein, iron and magnesium. It has an almond butter dressing with not a drop of mayo in sight.

Serves 10

Preparation time: 10 minutes, plus 2 hours chilling

500g (1lb 2oz) white cabbage

1 red pepper, seeds and core removed

3 carrots

4 tbsp rice wine vinegar

4 tbsp almond butter

1½ tbsp lemon juice, plus extra to taste

2 tbsp coconut nectar

1 tsp salt, plus extra for salting

1 tsp toasted sesame oil

2 tsp tamari

125g (4½oz) dry-toasted peanuts, coarsely chopped, to serve

Finely shred the vegetables in a food processor.

Combine the rest of the ingredients except the peanuts in a mixing bowl, stirring until the sauce has a thick texture similar to mayonnaise.

Salt the shredded vegetables, pour the dressing slowly over them and toss them several times. You want the salad to be well dressed, but not drenched in dressing. Set aside and refrigerate for at least 2 hours before serving.

Add a little lemon juice if needed before serving scattered with the chopped peanuts.

Roasted Cassava & Green Sauce

Cassava is a New World food that's been around for more than 10,000 years. It's a staple food in Brazil, Paraguay and Indonesia. This vegetable root is loaded with beneficial dietary fibre, which helps to reduce blood pressure and cholesterol levels and supports stable blood sugar. It's rich in magnesium, copper, manganese, folate and vitamin C. All in all, eating this healthy root will help keep you nutritionally balanced.

Serves 4

Preparation time: 5 minutes, plus 35 minutes cooking

1kg (2lb 4oz) cassava, peeled, stringy centre removed, flesh cut into 2cm (¾in) x 12cm (4½in) sticks

olive oil

salt

Green Sauce (*see* page 66), to serve

Preheat the oven to 200°C (400°F), Gas Mark 7.

Bring a large saucepan of water to the boil, salt the water well and add the cassava sticks. Cook for about 18 minutes.

Drain and arrange the sticks on a baking tray. Season generously with salt and olive oil and bake until golden; about15 minutes.

Serve with Green Sauce on the side or on the top.

Note
Never eat cassava raw; it should always be cooked before eating.

A selection of naturally delicious desserts. From laid-back sundaes to the best macadamia cookies in the world, there are plenty of sweets here to fall in love with.

Desserts

Raw Chocolate Tart

This tart is sweetened only with dates. Cacao is known as the food of the gods for good reason. It's packed with antioxidants, high in magnesium and protein and contains many vitamins and minerals. It's also an aphrodisiac and balances hormone swings. The hazelnuts are rich in good fats and support heart, brain and skin health, making this a naturally mood-enhancing dessert.

Serves 9

Preparation time: 15 minutes, plus 6 hours refrigeration

For the date paste

350g (12oz) Medjool dates, pitted

125ml (4fl oz) water

For the hazelnut crust

90g (3¼oz) hazelnuts

35g (1¼oz) desiccated coconut

3 tbsp cacao powder

3 tbsp cacao nibs

pinch of salt

175g (6oz) dates, pitted, plus extra if needed

For the chocolate filling

250g (9oz) cashew nuts, soaked overnight, then drained

300g (10½oz) date paste (*see* above)

1 tsp vanilla extract

¼ tsp salt

225ml (8fl oz) water

125g (4½oz) cacao powder

100g (3½oz) coconut oil

Fruit Chia Jam (*see* page 72), to serve

Start by preparing the date paste. Combine the dates and water in a food processor. Blend until very smooth, scraping down the sides of the processor to make sure the dates are well incorporated. Store in an airtight container in the refrigerator for up to 2 weeks.

To make the crust, put all the ingredients except the dates into a food processor and blend until well combined. Add the dates little by little while blending; the mixture should hold together but be easy to break up. If it is too dry, add more dates. Press the mixture into an 18cm (7in) square springform or loose-based cake tin lined with baking parchment and put in the refrigerator while you make the filling.

To make the filling, blend together all the ingredients except the cacao powder and coconut oil until smooth. Add the cacao powder and coconut oil and blend until well incorporated. Then pour on to the crust, covering it evenly.

Refrigerate for 6 hours or overnight. If you are short of time you can put the tart in the freezer so that it sets faster. It can also be stored in the freezer for up to 1 month. Try eating it frozen too – it tastes great.

Serve cut into 9 squares topped with Fruit Chia Jam.

Banoffee Pie

This healthy, raw pie is based on one of our classic restaurant desserts. It is a show-stopping dessert that's great for a lunch or supper party. This recipe is naturally sweet, sugar-free and nut-free – and made for sharing.

Serves 8

Preparation time: 20 minutes, plus 30 minutes refrigeration and overnight chilling for the coconut cream

For the cookie base

215g (7½oz) gluten-free rolled oats

100g (3½oz) desiccated coconut

¼ tsp vanilla powder

pinch of salt

1 tsp lemon juice

125ml (4fl oz) maple syrup, or other sweetener

For the maca caramel sauce

250g (9oz) Medjool dates, soaked in warm water for 15 minutes

5 tbsp water

1 tsp lemon juice

1 tsp maca powder (optional)

3 ripe bananas, cut into 0.5cm (¼in) slices

cacao nibs, to garnish (optional)

For the coconut whipped cream

2 x 400ml (14fl oz) cans coconut cream, refrigerated overnight

2 tbsp raw honey or other sweetener (use a clear sweetener to keep the white colour)

1 tsp vanilla extract

To make the cookie base, line a 20cm (8in) loose-based tart tin with baking parchment. Put the oats, coconut, vanilla powder and salt into a food processor and blend until the mixture has the texture of flour.

Add the lemon juice and maple syrup and blend until combined. Transfer into the lined tart tin, pressing the mixture down firmly with your fingers or the back of a spoon on the base and the sides of the tin. Chill in the refrigerator while you make the filling.

For the caramel sauce, place the drained dates in a food processor or blender with the water, lemon juice and maca powder (if using) and blend until you have a smooth, velvety, caramel-like mixture.

Take the base out of the freezer and top with the caramel layer. Smooth it down with a spatula or the back of a spoon. Arrange the banana slices on top. Put it back in the refrigerator to chill while you make the cream.

Take the chilled coconut cream cans out of the refrigerator. Carefully scoop the thick layer of solid coconut cream at the top of the cans into a bowl, leaving the liquid behind. Add the honey or other sweetener and the vanilla extract. Use an electric whisk to whip the cream until peaks form.

Take the pie out of the refrigerator and top with the whipped coconut cream. You can use a piping bag to pipe the cream on top or spoon it over the top and spread it out. Sprinkle some cacao nibs on top and serve immediately.

This dish is not suitable for freezing.

Notes

Coconut cream will make a larger quantity of coconut whipped cream than full-fat coconut milk because it contains more cream. It may be firm enough to separate without chilling first, depending on the brand. Only full-fat coconut milk will harden.

Laid-back Sundae

GF VG

Serves 9
Preparation time: 40 minutes,
plus 5 hours freezing

250g (9oz) strawberries

For the vanilla ice cream
200g (7oz) raw cashews, soaked (*see* page 49),
then drained
125ml (4fl oz) water or unsweetened,
non-dairy milk
135ml (4¼fl oz) maple syrup
8 tbsp unscented coconut oil
2 tsp vanilla extract
1 tsp raw ground vanilla (or scrape the seeds
from ½ vanilla pod)
½ tsp salt

For the chocolate brownie
2 tbsp ground flaxseed
5 tbsp water
50g (1¾oz) chocolate (100 per cent cocoa),
melted
7½ tbsp coconut oil, plus extra for the tin
100g (3½oz) coconut sugar
4 tbsp coconut nectar
1 tsp vanilla extract
¾ tsp gluten-free baking powder
pinch of salt
60g (2¼oz) cacao powder
60g (2¼oz) buckwheat flour
60g (2¼oz) rice flour
25g (1oz) ground almonds (or tigernut flour
for nut-free version)
60g (2¼oz) chocolate chips

For the caramelized pecans
50g (1¾oz) pecans
1½ tbsp maple syrup

For the caramel sauce
55g (2oz) coconut butter (from the bottom
of the jar, rather than the oily top layer)
135ml (4¼fl oz) maple syrup
2 tbsp coconut oil
½ tsp vanilla extract

'OMG!' is the usual exclamation when people first eat it. Vanilla is a truly medicinal food that has been used for centuries. It enhances brain health and mood, as well as being a great source of magnesium, potassium and calcium *and* being an aphrodisiac. This recipe contains no refined sugars, can be nut-free and uses ground flaxseed instead of eggs. Enjoy!

Place the ice cream ingredients in a blender and blend until smooth. Transfer to a freezer-proof container and freeze for 5–6 hours or overnight.

Next make the brownies. Preheat the oven to 180°C (350°F), Gas Mark 4. Lightly oil an 18cm (7in) square cake tin and line it with greaseproof paper. Mix the flaxseed and water in a small bowl. Set aside for 15 minutes.

Melt the chocolate and coconut oil in a heatproof bowl over a saucepan of boiling water. Scrape into a large bowl with the coconut sugar, nectar and vanilla extract. Whisk to combine. Add the flaxseeds and whisk again. Then add the baking powder, salt and cacao powder and whisk once more.

Add the flours and almond meal or tigernut flour and fold in with a spatula until just mixed. Then add the chocolate chips.

Pour the batter into the prepared tin and bake for 20 minutes or until the edges appear dry and slightly fluffy and the centre is no longer wet. Remove from the oven and cool in the tin for 15 minutes before gently lifting out. Once cool, slice into squares.

While the brownies are cooking, prepare the pecans by coating them in maple syrup. Place them on a baking sheet lined with greaseproof paper and bake in the oven for 10 minutes until toasted. Take out and set aside to cool.

For the sauce, melt the coconut butter in a heatproof bowl over a saucepan of boiling water. Add the maple syrup, coconut oil and vanilla and stir well to combine, then set aside.

To assemble, place a spoonful of sauce in each bowl, top with cubes of brownie, scoops of ice cream, some caramelized pecans and strawberries. Drizzle with more caramel sauce and serve.

The brownies will stay fresh in an airtight container for up to 3 days and will keep in the freezer for up to 1 month. Pour any leftover caramel sauce into moulds and put into the refrigerator to set into coconut fudge.

White Macadamia Cookies

These cookies are delicious at any time of the day. Macadamia nuts are high in vitamin A, iron and protein, and these cookies are free from refined sugar and grains – and also paleo-friendly. The only problem will be eating just one! We love them dipped in a nut-milk drink or as a cosy evening snack when watching a movie. They are crumbly and so delicious that it's hard to stop eating them.

Makes 16
Preparation time: 30 minutes

1½ tbsp chia seeds

3¾ tablespoons water

150g (5½oz) ground almonds

40g (1½oz) coconut flour

150g (5½oz) coconut sugar

140g (5oz) cashew butter (or other nut butter)

100g (3½oz) coconut oil

2 tsp gluten-free baking powder

1 tbsp vanilla extract

pinch of salt

30g (1oz) macadamia nuts

85g (3oz) vegan white chocolate chips

Mix the chia seeds with the water and leave for 5–10 minutes until the seeds have absorbed all the water and have become gelatinous.

Put all the other ingredients except the nuts and chocolate chips into a food processor. Whizz together until well combined. Add the nuts and chocolate chips and mix them in with a wooden spoon until well dispersed.

Use an ice cream scoop to measure out balls of cookie dough, placing them on a baking tray lined with greaseproof paper and flattening them with your hands into cookie shapes. Put the tray in the refrigerator until they are completely set and cold and preheat the oven to 180°C (350°F), Gas Mark 4.

Bake the chilled cookies for 15 minutes until golden. They will feel a little soft when you take them out of the oven but will harden as they cool.

Allow the cookies to sit for 5 minutes to cool and harden, then transfer them to a cooling rack until completely cold.

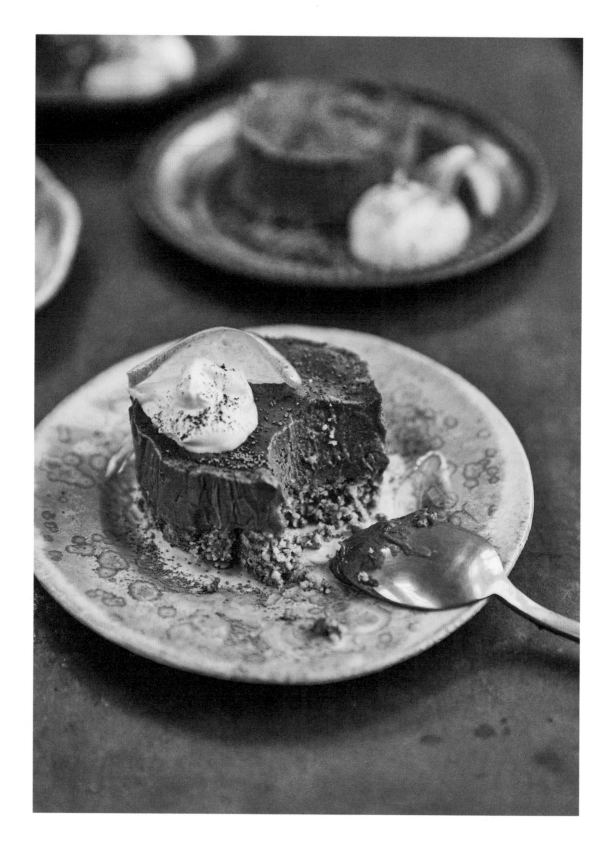

Matcha Lime Avocado Cakes

These nut-free cakes are full of healthy fats and proteins. A creamy and light combination of matcha, lime and avocado blended together to create a zingy taste sensation. Pumpkin seeds are an excellent source of magnesium and zinc, helping to support the heart and immune system, and the matcha supplies good levels of antioxidants, as well as working as a metabolism booster. This is a great dessert to share, bringing colour and healthy flavours to the table.

Serves 4

Preparation time: 15 minutes, plus 5 hours freezing

For the crust
100g (3½oz) raw pumpkin seeds
4 soft Medjool dates, pitted
½ tbsp coconut oil

For the matcha filling
I avocado, pitted
4 tbsp lime juice
4 tbsp maple syrup
1 tbsp coconut oil
zest of 1 lime
1 tsp vanilla extract
1 tbsp matcha powder
4 tbsp full-fat coconut milk
pinch of salt

To serve
150ml (¼ pint) coconut yogurt
matcha powder, for sprinkling
1 lime, thinly sliced

Put all the crust ingredients into a food processor and blend into a fine, sticky crumble. Split this mixture between 4 round moulds (or 4 holes of a muffin tin) and press to form a flat, even base. Put the moulds or muffin tin in the freezer while you make the filling.

Put all the filling ingredients into a blender and whizz at high speed until smooth. Take the moulds out of the freezer and spoon the mixture on top of the prepared crusts, smoothing out the tops.

Return to the freezer for at least 3 hours, or overnight, to set. If frozen overnight, take the moulds out of the freezer about 1 hour before serving.

Serve with a dollop of coconut yogurt, a sprinkling of sifted matcha powder and lime slices.

Fig Tarte Tatin

GF VG (if honey not used)

When we were testing recipes for this book, our friend Paul came to the house carrying a basket of figs fresh from the tree. Being a warm and friendly team, we happily accepted his offer to make us a dessert. When we first tasted his tarte, we knew the recipe had to be in the book. Once you've tried it, you'll be hooked too. Figs are a rich source of minerals, including magnesium and calcium and are also powerful antioxidants. This is a delicious dessert with no refined sugar or gluten – a summer delight.

Serves 12
Preparation time: 50 minutes

For the crust
175g (6oz) buckwheat flour, plus a little extra for rolling out
85g (3oz) ground almonds
115g (4oz) coconut sugar
1 tbsp ground flaxseed
2½ tbsp water
70g (2½oz) coconut butter
3–4 tbsp almond milk
zest of 1 lemon
pinch of salt

For the topping
1 tbsp coconut butter
2 tbsp coconut sugar
450g (1lb) figs, quartered

For the coconut cream
400ml (14fl oz) full-fat coconut milk
1 tbsp honey or other sweetener
½ tsp vanilla extract

Preheat the oven to 180°C (350°F), Gas Mark 4.

To make the crust, put the buckwheat flour and almond flour into a bowl with the coconut sugar and stir until combined. Mix the flaxseed with the water and add to the bowl along with the coconut butter, then slowly pour in the almond milk. Stir until the mixture has a doughy consistency. Wrap the bowl in a clean tea towel and place it in the refrigerator for 30 minutes.

Next, make the topping. Smear a round 30cm (12in) dish (ideally a clay dish) with the coconut butter. Pour the coconut sugar evenly over the coconut butter. Arrange the figs over the base.

Spread a little buckwheat flour over a clean surface and roll out the dough until it is about 8.5mm (⅓in) thick and a little larger than the dish. Slice the dough into quarters and place the quarters on top of the figs until they are all covered. Once you've covered the figs, smooth the pastry quarters into each other and tuck the edges down the side of the dish.

Place in the oven and cook for 30 minutes until golden brown on top. When you are ready to serve, place a plate on top of the dish, holding it against the dish, and turn the dish upside down so the figs are on top.

Make the coconut cream by blending all the ingredients together until well combined.

To serve, cut into 12 slices and drizzle each with coconut cream.

Pitaya Tart

This is the prettiest pink tart we've ever seen. Pitaya is also known as dragon fruit. It is loaded with nutrients, including vitamin C, calcium and phytonutrients and is also rich in antioxidants. This raw, intensely colourful tart is quick to make and will look stunning on any table.

Serves 12
Preparation time: 15 minutes, plus 5 hours freezing

For the crust
140g (5oz) almonds
6 dates
30g (1oz) coconut flour
¼ tsp vanilla powder
2 tbsp coconut oil, melted
pinch of salt

For the filling
260g (9½oz) cashews, soaked (*see* page 49)
200g (7oz) frozen pitaya
1½ tsp lemon juice
4 tbsp maple syrup
½ tsp vanilla extract
pinch of salt
2 tbsp coconut oil, melted
blackberries and blueberries, to serve

To make the crust, put the nuts and the dates in a food processor and blend until they are broken down and combined. Add the rest of the crust ingredients and process until well combined.

Line a 20cm (8in) round tart tin with greaseproof paper and fill it with the crust, pressing it down to form an even layer over the base and up the sides. Put it in the freezer while you prepare the filling.

For the filling, rinse the cashews and drain them well. Put in a blender with all the other ingredients except the coconut oil. Blend until you have a smooth consistency. Then slowly pour in the coconut oil, still blending.

Take the tart tin out of the freezer and pour the filling over the crust. Return to the freezer for about 3 hours, until set.

Take the tart out of the freezer and defrost for 20 minutes at room temperature (or 1 hour in the refrigerator) before serving with the purple berries.

This will keep in the freezer for up to 1 month.

Chocolate Wheels

Makes 20

**Preparation time: 40 minutes,
  plus 30 minutes refrigeration**

150g (5½oz) Raspberry Chia Jam (*see* page 72)

For the biscuit

70g (2½oz) shredded coconut

70g (2½oz) ground almonds

85g (3oz) cashews or macadamia nuts

2 tbsp coconut butter

4 tbsp maple syrup

½ tsp vanilla powder

For the coconut marshmallow

55g (2oz) coconut butter

3 tbsp liquid coconut oil

90g (3¼oz) coconut cream, or fat from
  the top of a can of full-fat coconut milk
  chilled overnight

½ tsp vanilla extract

1½ tbsp maple syrup

For the chocolate coating

35g (1¼oz) cacao butter

60g (2¼oz) cacao powder

4 tbsp liquid coconut oil

2½ tbsp maple syrup

Alternatively, melt 150g (5½oz) dairy-free
  dark chocolate (72 per cent cocoa) if you
  don't want to make the chocolate yourself

This is the Farmacy version of the iconic Wagon Wheel biscuit. But these have a healthy edge. They taste gorgeous, with layers of fruity chia jam, coconut marshmallow and cacao chocolate. Grown-up kids and real kids love these. They are great for parties, snacks and to share from a lunchbox. You will need a 6cm (2½in) cookie cutter for this recipe.

To prepare the biscuit, put the shredded coconut, ground almonds and cashews or macadamia nuts into a food processor and pulse until you have a fine texture. Soften the coconut butter by putting the jar in hot water, then add 2 tablespoons to the food processor, along with the maple syrup and vanilla powder, and pulse until well combined.

Turn out the mixture and form it into a ball, then roll out on baking paper until it is about 1cm (½in) thick. Cut out the biscuits with a round cookie cutter until you have used all the dough. Put on a tray and place in the freezer while you make the other components.

For the coconut marshmallow, put all the ingredients in a blender and whizz until smooth and creamy. Place in the refrigerator for 10 minutes.

To make the chocolate coating, melt the cacao butter in a heatproof bowl over a saucepan of boiling water. Add the other ingredients and stir together until smooth and silky. Alternatively, if you are using shop-bought chocolate, melt the chocolate.

To assemble, spread a layer of marshmallow on one of the biscuits, followed by a layer of jam. Top with another biscuit. Repeat until you have used all the biscuits.

Dunk each biscuit sandwich in the bowl of melted chocolate using 2 forks, then place on a tray lined with baking paper. Put in the refrigerator for 30 minutes until the chocolate is set.

These biscuits will last for 10 days in an airtight container in the refrigerator. They can be frozen for up to a month. When frozen, remove from the freezer 10 minutes before eating, to allow them to soften slightly.

Chocolate & Almond Nice Cream

Regulars at Farmacy know we love a nice cream. It was hard to choose which flavour to include. Emily loves this banana and almond version and could quite happily eat it every day. It has a creamy edge and chocolate fudge chunks in the middle. There are no grains in the recipe and no flour, and it is sweetened with natural sugars. All the ingredients support good health. This is a nice cream your body won't mind you eating.

Serves 6–8 servings
**Preparation time: 15 minutes,
    plus 4 hours freezing**

For the fudge

50g (1¾oz) coconut flour

3 tbsp cacao powder

6 tbsp maple syrup

¾ tsp vanilla extract

pinch of salt

For the ice cream

6 peeled, sliced and frozen bananas (you can use fresh but these take longer to set)

175g (6oz) smooth Almond Butter (*see* page 74)

3 tbsp maple syrup

1 tsp vanilla extract

Put all the fudge ingredients into a small food processor and blend until well combined. The mixture should resemble dry brownie pieces. Turn into a bowl and break up the mixture into chunks or finer pieces if desired.

Put all the ice cream ingredients into a blender and whizz at a high speed until completely smooth. Transfer the mixture into a freezer-proof container. Add the fudge pieces, folding them in with a spoon until they are evenly distributed. Freeze for 4–5 hours until set.

Here are some of our favourite natural recipes for keeping your home and body healthy without using chemicals or toxic ingredients. We use natural ingredients in these home and beauty preparations. Ditch store-bought products in favour of those you make at home, so you can be sure they are chemical-free and organic; good for you, good for your purse and kind to the planet.

Home & Beauty

Body Beautiful Scrub

VG

This easy recipe uses natural ingredients to exfoliate the skin and keep it glowing and healthy. You can use it daily, or weekly for a more intense scrub. As it's homemade, you can be sure there are no chemicals or nasties in there.

Makes 250ml (9fl oz)
Preparation time: 5 minutes

85g (3oz) granulated sugar (we use coconut sugar)

100g (3½oz) coconut oil

1 tsp vanilla powder, or your favourite essential oil (optional)

Combine all the ingredients and put in a glass container with a sealable lid. Lasts for months stored in a cool place.

How to use

Rub gently on your skin while in the shower. Massage and rinse.

Edible Body Butter

We love using natural ingredients like these to keep skin glowing, smooth and healthy. Skin is the biggest organ of the body and it doesn't help to cover it in chemicals. Love your body; use natural preparations. You can eat this too – it's a versatile and fun-to-use body butter.

Makes 480ml (17fl oz)
Preparation time: 15 minutes

225g (8oz) cacao butter
200g (7oz) coconut oil
a few drops of your favourite essential oil,
   such as rose (optional)

Put the cacao butter and coconut oil in a heatproof glass dish over a bowl of hot water to melt. Once melted, mix with any oil you like. Pour into a beautiful container.

Lasts for 3 months stored in a cool place.

How to use

Apply to the whole body for wonderful hydration and moisture.

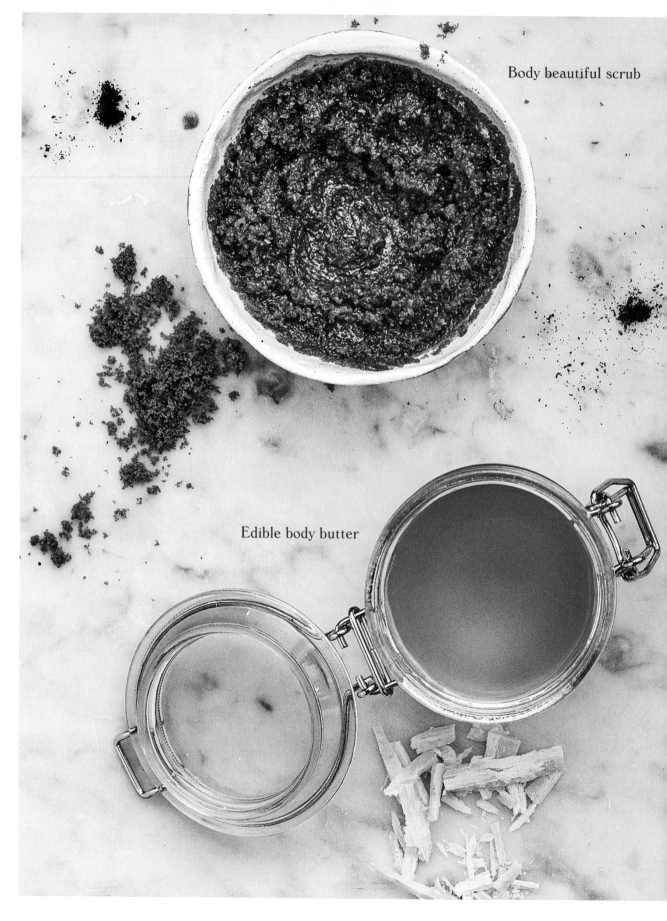

Body beautiful scrub

Edible body butter

Natural body wash

Oat & honey
face cleanser

Natural Body Wash

The cleansers we put on our skin every day are important and many body washes are loaded with chemicals. Castile soap is a pure, natural, plant-based soap that is gentle on the skin. It's one of the best biodegradable soaps that can be made by hand. This recipe gives you a pure and safe body wash to keep your skin clean and looking healthy and radiant.

Makes 700ml (1¼ pints)
Preparation time: 5 minutes

60ml (4 tbsp) liquid Castile soap
700ml (1¼ pints) water
25g (1oz) oatmeal
3 drops tea tree oil
3 drops peppermint essential oil

Mix all the ingredients together and store in a screw-top jar.

Oat & Honey Face Cleanser

Here's a simple, natural recipe for cleansing your skin, leaving it feeling fresh and cared for. Many over-the-counter cleansers are loaded with preservatives and strong ingredients that we don't want to use on our faces. This cleanser is made with oats, which are anti-inflammatory and perfect for all skin types, including sensitive skins. Honey is antibacterial and full of antioxidants, while also helping to nourish and cleanse the skin.

Makes 125ml (4fl oz)
Preparation time: 15 minutes

25g (1oz) rolled oats

2 tbsp honey

2 tbsp sweet almond, coconut or olive oil, plus extra if needed

Grind the rolled oats into a fine powder in a coffee grinder, blender or food processor. The texture should be soft and powdery.

Transfer the powder to a bowl and mix with the rest of the ingredients until you have a thick, sticky mixture. If it's too sticky or clumpy, add a little extra oil.

Store in an airtight container.

How to use

Wet your face with warm water. Place a small amount (less than 1 teaspoon) of the mixture in your hands and rub them together. Massage the mixture on to your skin in a circular motion, rubbing gently for a couple of minutes. You can leave this on for 5–10 minutes for deep pore cleansing. Wash off with warm water and pat your skin dry.

Detox Face Mask

From time to time, everyone's face can use a little extra loving care. This is our go-to recipe for a great face mask treatment using pure and natural ingredients. You can use this weekly or whenever you feel you need a beauty boost. The clay and charcoal naturally draw out impurities from the skin. The honey has antibacterial properties and chlorella helps to promote cell regeneration and brighten the complexion. You can buy clay, charcoal powder and chlorella from health food stores and chemists.

Makes 2 face masks
Preparation time: 5 minutes

2 tsp water
1 tsp bentonite clay
1 tsp activated charcoal powder
¼ tsp chlorella powder
½ tsp raw honey

Put the water into a small glass bowl and sprinkle the clay over the top. Allow the clay to absorb the water for about 10 seconds, then add the other ingredients. This makes the mixture easier to combine.

Use a small rubber spatula to mash and mix everything together. You may need to mix for a few minutes to remove lumps from the clay.

This mask doesn't store well as there are no preservatives.

How to use

Apply the mask liberally to your face. Allow to dry for about 10 minutes before washing off with warm water.

Fresh Breath Rinse

This mouth rinse helps to care for teeth and gums, as well as supporting the remineralization of teeth. It's also effective in helping to reduce inflammation or irritation of the gums and teeth. Salt water helps to keep the mouth healthy and neutralizes the pH (acidity) of saliva. Use this every day to help keep your mouth, gums and teeth in great shape.

Makes 500ml (18fl oz)
Preparation time: 5 minutes

4 tsp pure salt, such as Himalayan or Celtic
500ml (18fl oz) boiling water
2 drops food grade peppermint essential oil

Place the salt in a glass screw-top jar and pour the water over it. Add the peppermint oil.

Put the lid on the jar and shake it to dissolve some of the salt. It will dissolve further over a few days.

Lasts for 1 month stored in a cool place.

How to use

Use before and after brushing your teeth. Take a mouthful, swish it around your mouth and spit it out. Do not swallow.

Natural Toothpaste

This is a natural alternative to commercial toothpastes without harmful ingredients. Some high-street brands use fluoride in toothpaste, which is highly toxic; avoid these. Check the ingredients in your toothpaste carefully. Better still, make your own so you know what's in it. This recipe has natural cleansing power. The coconut oil helps to get rid of toxins and keep teeth naturally white and clean as well as being antibacterial and antimicrobial. Baking soda neutralizes the acid-loving bacteria in your mouth which are responsible for causing cavities. It also helps to whiten teeth, remove plaque and maintain healthy gums. Peppermint oil is also antibacterial.

Makes 4 tbsp
Preparation time: 5 minutes

4 tbsp coconut oil, preferably unscented
1½ tbsp baking soda
10–15 drops food grade peppermint essential oil
5 drops myrrh extract (optional)
2 drops liquid stevia, to sweeten (optional)

Put the coconut oil in a small saucepan and soften it over a low heat. Remove from the heat and allow to cool slightly. Mix in the other ingredients and stir well.

Once the mixture has solidified, give it another stir, as the baking soda may have settled at the bottom.

Store in a glass jar with a sealed lid. Lasts for 3 months in a sealed jar in a cool place.

How to use

Use twice daily on a wet toothbrush for healthy and clean teeth and mouth.

Love Earth Home Cleaner

House cleaning products can be quite toxic, especially those that contain perfumes, strong chemicals and bleach. This is a recipe for a general-purpose cleaner which you can use to clean surfaces and remove water deposit stains on shower panels, chrome bathroom fittings, windows, bathroom mirrors and so on. It's a versatile, non-harmful cleaner that keeps your house fresh and free of toxic sprays and harsh chemical agents. You will need a spray bottle to store it in.

Makes 2 litres
Preparation time: 5 minutes

125ml (4fl oz) apple cider vinegar
50g (1¾oz) baking soda
2 litres (3½ pints) water
juice of 1 lemon

Mix all the ingredients together and pour into a spray bottle.

Index

Cookery Notes

Key to nutritional info recipe codes:

GF = gluten free

NF = nut free

R = raw

VG = vegan

Standard level spoon measurements are used in all recipes.

1 tablespoon = one 15ml spoon

1 teaspoon = one 5ml spoon

Fresh herbs should be used unless otherwise stated.

Ovens should be preheated to the specific temperature – if using
a fan-assisted oven, follow manufacturer's instructions for adjusting
the time and the temperature.

Salt should be sea salt flakes unless otherwise stated. See page 41
for more on salt.

Pepper should be freshly ground black pepper unless otherwise stated.

Honey should be raw and can be substituted in any recipes for coconut
nectar or maple syrup to keep it vegan.

All nuts should be raw and unsalted, unless stated otherwise.

Water should always be filtered.

This book includes dishes made with nuts and nut derivatives.
It is advisable for those with known allergic reactions to nuts and
nut derivatives and those who may be potentially vulnerable to these
allergies, such as pregnant and nursing mothers, older people, babies
and young children, to avoid dishes made with nuts and nut oils.
It is also prudent to check the labels of pre-prepared ingredients
for the possible inclusion of nut derivatives.

We regularly update our website with details of stockists that may help
you when it comes to sourcing some of the more unusual ingredients
used in our recipes.

Acknowledgements

The Farmacy team have worked together combining their skills and knowledge to create a new vision for plant-based food. This collaboration of understanding comes from many years of discovery in eating and living consciously.

We would like to extend a heartfelt thank you to everyone who has been a part of the creative process, allowing us to bring health and happiness to your kitchen.

The team gives thanks to Camilla Fayed for leading the way with her vision for Farmacy and the first Farmacy recipe book. Camilla and Susie Pearl worked closely to bring the concept of Farmacy Kitchen from an idea into this beautiful book, along with the great food team.

Thanks to Pietro Cuevas and Emily Pearson for creating delicious food combinations and innovative recipes. Thanks to Emma Newman for being the backbone of the project, whose invaluable assistance enabled us to bring this book to life.